THE MARSHALL CAVENDISH
☆ ☆ ☆ ILLUSTRATED ☆ ☆ ☆
ENCYCLOPEDIA OF
WORLD WAR II

VOLUME 17

THE MARSHALL CAVENDISH
☆ ☆ ☆ ILLUSTRATED ☆ ☆ ☆
ENCYCLOPEDIA OF
WORLD WAR II

Based on the original text by
Lieutenant Colonel Eddy Bauer

CONSULTANT EDITOR

Brigadier General James L. Collins, Jr., U.S.A.
CHIEF OF MILITARY HISTORY,
DEPARTMENT OF THE ARMY

MARSHALL CAVENDISH CORPORATION/NEW YORK

CONTENTS

Chapter 144 The Allies Confer 2241

THE QUEBEC CONFERENCE
Occupied Germany
The Morgenthau Plan
Churchill's opinion alters
Eisenhower's view: "silly and criminal"
German propaganda benefits

THE MOSCOW CONFERENCE
Churchill's initiative
Spheres of influence
Tito goes it alone
Eden versus Molotov
Poles in exile
Combined Polish government?
Conduct of the war
Violate Swiss neutrality?
Germany to be divided

THE YALTA CONFERENCE
Stalin recognises the "Lublin Committee"
The new government moves in
The conference opens
Roosevelt chosen as Chairman
American vacillation
Formidable negotiator
Churchill's difficult position
The resolutions

Chapter 145 Himmler's Offensive 2269

Himmler's offensive
de Gaulle disapproves
Churchill sides with de Gaulle
The battle for Strasbourg
The German defence
The Colman pocket wiped out
Montgomery and Eisenhower clash again
Support for Eisenhower

Chapter 146 Remagen Bridge 2282

Rundstedt powerless
Allied superiority
Complete surprise
No retreat
Triumphant advance
Surprise crossing

Chapter 147 Across the Rhine 2297

Kesselring caught off balance
To surrender or not?
Scorched earth policy
Montgomery prepares to cross the Rhine
The battle begins
Airborne landings
Large bridgehead
Eisenhower's excellent plan
Collapse of the German 15th Army
The Ruhr pocket
Eisenower gives up the idea of Berlin
Stalin approves warmly
Churchill objects violently
Eisenhower refuses to countermand
   his orders

Chapter 148 The End in Italy......... 2325

Superb defences
Revised plans
The offensive falters
Coriano ridge taken
Winter war
Command shuffles
The last lap

Chapter 149 Germany: The Trap Closes 2353

Montgomery drives for Lubeck
Hamburg and Bremen taken
Canadians in Holland
Last German high command change
More French advances
Patch moves south-east
Berchtesgaden taken

Chapter 150 The Battle of
Lake Balaton 2371
The Russian riposte
Vienna falls
The defence of Berlin
Roosevelt dies
The final appeal

Editorial Director: Brian Innes
Editor-in-chief: Brigadier Peter Young, D.S.O., M.C., M.A.
Managing Director: Richard Humble
Editor: Christopher Chant
Art Editor: Jim Bridge

The QUEBEC Conference

n Tuesday September 6, 1944, Churchill
nd his three chiefs-of-staff left the Clyde
n board the liner *Queen Mary* for
alifax, Nova Scotia. Here a special
ain took them to Quebec late in
e morning of September 11. President
oosevelt and his military colleagues
ere waiting for the British party. To
inston Churchill's great disappoint-
ent Harry Hopkins had excused himlf: apart from the health reasons which
plained his absence (and these were
al enough), he was also suffering the
nsequences of his loss of favour at the
hite House at this time.

During this Anglo-American con-
rence, which had been named "Octa-
n", the discussion concerned mainly
e form of participation to be taken by
e British forces in the fight against
pan, after the Third Reich had been
iven to unconditional surrender. Plan-
ng included operations in Burma, a
ssible air and naval offensive from
ustralia against Singapore, and putting
Royal Navy formation under the command of the American Pacific Fleet,
which had just won a victory at the
Marianas Islands and was about to win
another at Leyte.

In the European theatre, it was decided
not to withdraw a single division from
the Allied forces in the Mediterranean
until the result of the attack the 15th
Army Group was preparing to launch
across the Apennines was known; its
objective was the Adige line, just short of
the Piave.

Occupied Germany

An agreement was also made between the
British and the Americans to mark off
their future occupation zones in Germany. After some argument about the
allocation of the Westphalian industrial
basin, it was decided, according to Admiral Leahy, President Roosevelt's Chief-
of-Staff, to divide the zones as follows:
"(a) The British forces, under a British

△ *British troops in combat against the Japanese in the Burmese jungle. Operations in this theatre were among the points discussed at Quebec.*
▷ *The highly strategic Burma Road, cutting through the jungle terrain. This was the route by which General Chiang Kai-shek Japanese conquest of Burma in 1942 closed the road, and the Americans subsequently supplied the Chinese by air lift.*

commander, will occupy Germany west of the Rhine and east of the Rhine north of a line from Coblenz following the northern border of Hessen and Nassau to the border of the area allocated to the Soviet Government.

(b) The forces of the United States, under a United States commander, will occupy Germany east of the Rhine, south of the line from Coblenz following the northern border of Hessen–Nassau and west of the area allocated to the Soviet Government.

(c) Control of the ports of Bremen and Bremerhaven and the necessary staging areas in that immediate vicinity will be vested in the commander of the American zone.

(d) American area to have, in addition, access through the western and north-western seaports and passage through the British controlled area.

(e) Accurate delineation of the above outlined British and American areas of control can be made at a later date."

Reading this text one notices that:
1. at this time no French occupation zone was provided for;
2. Bremen and Bremerhaven were included in the American occupation zone because President Roosevelt wa ted to make sure that his troops wou be supplied without using French ter tory; and
3. Berlin was not mentioned and the was no reference to the faciliti which the two Western powers wou require from their Soviet ally if th were to have free access to the Germ capital at all times.

Robert Murphy, the American diplom who had just taken up his duties adviser to General Eisenhower on G man affairs, frequently mentioned a deplored this last point. He states in h memoirs that "no provision had be made for the Anglo-American powers reach that city", and notes that h colleague James Riddleberger, the Sta Department's delegate to the Europe Consultative Council in London, who w equally aware of this omission, ha suggested that "the occupation zon should converge upon Berlin like slic of pie, thus providing each zone with own frontage in the capital city". Murp also asked Riddleberger whom he ha approached with his plan. The latt had told Ambassador Winant, who h been opposed to any modification of th original plan and accused Riddleberger of not having confidence in Soviet Russia. Riddleberger replied that on this he was exactly right.

In addition, according to Murphy, the "daydreams" of Winant, the U.S. Ambassador in London, and therefore the American representative for Russo-American affairs at the European Consultative Council, relied too much on Roosevelt's usual formula: "I can handle Stalin."

The Morgenthau Plan

During the "Octagon" Conference the notorious Morgenthau Plan (named after its author, the Secretary of the Treasury), which dealt with the treatment of Germany after its defeat, was endorsed by the British and American Governments.

Since the beginning of August, Eisenhower had been requesting instructions on the attitude to be adopted after the German defeat, and the War Department sent him a note on the subject, asking him to make his observations. However, a member of Eisenhower's staff committed the double indiscretion of getting hold of a copy of this memorandum and sending it to Henry Morgenthau. Morgenthau had wormed his way into the President's favour to such an extent that he was the only member of his cabinet to call him by his first name.

After the cabinet session of August 26, 1944, James V. Forrestal, the Secretary of the Navy, noted in his valuable diary:

"The Secretary of the Treasury (Henry Morgenthau, Jr.) came in with the President with whom he had had lunch. The President said that he had been talking with the Secretary of the Treasury on the general question of the control of Germany after the end of the war. He said that he had just heard about a paper prepared by the Army and that he was not at all satisfied with the severity of the measures proposed. He said that the Germans should have simply a subsistence level of food—as he put it, soup kitchens would be ample to sustain life—that otherwise they should be stripped clean and should not have a level of subsistence above the lowest level of the people they had conquered.

"The Secretary of War (Henry L. Stimson) demurred from this view, but the President continued in the expression of

△ The principal military participants in the "Octagon" Conference. Discussion here included the part Britain was to play in the war against Japan, and initial agreement was reached over Allied occupation zones in post-war Germany.

▽ Henry Morgenthau Jr., U.S. Secretary of the Treasury and author of the Morgenthau Plan for the treatment of Germany after the war. In this, German factories were to be dismantled, mines flooded, raw materials cut off, and the people were to live by subsistence farming. At the conference, Churchill and Roosevelt endorsed this Plan.

this attitude and finally said he would name a committee composing State, War, and Treasury which would consider the problem of how to handle Germany along the lines that he had outlined, that this committee would consult the Navy whenever naval questions were involved."

According to the plan, Germany would not only have her factories, in particular her steel plants, dismantled, but all her raw material resources also cut off, because she would be permanently forbidden to mine coal and iron ore. Her mines were to be flooded and the German people would have to subsist on crops and cattle-breeding as in the early times of the Holy Roman Empire. Secretary of State Cordell Hull and Secretary of War Henry L. Stimson were firm in their objections, but Roosevelt remained obstinate and, leaving his diplomatic chief in Washington, took Morgenthau with him to the Quebec Conference. It is interesting to note the reception given by Churchill to this inhuman and preposterous project.

Churchill's opinion alters

In the volume of his memoirs entitled *Triumph and Tragedy,* which he wrote in 1953, Churchill tells us:

"At first I violently opposed this idea But the President, with Mr. Morgenthau for whom we had much to ask – was s insistent that in the end we agreed t consider it."

This is both true and false. There is n doubt that he recoiled when he learned of the Morgenthau plan, as Lord Mora heard him say on September 13 at the dinner of the Citadel Night, when the subject came up:

"I'm all for disarming Germany, bu we ought not to prevent her living decently. There are bonds between th working classes of all countries, and th English people will not stand for th policy you are advocating." And he i said to have muttered: "You canno indict a whole nation."

On the other hand, when Roosevelt an Morgenthau insisted, Churchill, in spite of what he said, not only promised them that he would examine the plan for reducing Germany to a pastoral existence but after it had been examined by Pro fessor Lindemann (later Lord Cherwell) put his signature to it on September 15 According to Lord Moran, Cherwell a Churchill's scientific adviser had per suaded the Prime Minister, explaining what he had not noticed at first sight, tha "the plan will save Britain from bank ruptcy by eliminating a dangerous com petitor".

5

6

1. General H. H. Arnold
2. Air Chief-Marshal Sir Charles Portal
3. General Sir Alan Brooke
4. Field-Marshal Sir John Dill
5. Admiral E. J. King
6. General G. C. Marshall
7. Admiral of the Fleet Sir Dudley Pound
8. Admiral W. D. Leahy

It is tempting to dismiss the versions of Churchill and his doctor out of hand, as they are contradictory. However, the evidence given by Anthony Eden, now Lord Avon, supports Lord Moran's version point by point; he writes:

"On the morning of September 15th I joined the Prime Minister and the President, who were by now in agreement in their approval of the plan. Cherwell had supported Morgenthau and their joint advocacy had prevailed. Large areas of the Ruhr and the Saar were to be stripped of their manufacturing industries and turned into agricultural lands. It was as if one were to take the Black Country and turn it into Devonshire. I did not like the plan, nor was I convinced that it was to our national advantage.

"I said so, and also suggested that Mr. Cordell Hull's opinion should be sought for. This was the only occasion I can remember when the Prime Minister showed impatience with my views before foreign representatives. He resented my criticism of something which he and the President had approved, not I am sure on his account, but on the President's."

Meanwhile, Cordell Hull, on whose territory Morgenthau was trespassing, and Stimson, who refused to admit defeat, were left behind in Washington. However, they did not relax their opposition to the Morgenthau plan and on September 18,

the deputy Secretary of War, John Mc-Cloy, also condemned it to Forrestal:

7

"In general the programme according to Mr. McCloy, called for the conscious destruction of the economy in Germany and the encouragement of a state of impoverishment and disorder. He said he felt the Army's role in any programme would be most difficult because the Army, by training and instinct, would naturally turn to the re-creation of order as soon as possible, whereas under this programme they apparently were to encourage the opposite."

Eisenhower's view: "silly and criminal"

8

McCloy was not exaggerating in interpreting the feeling of the U.S. high command as he did. Already in August, when Morgenthau had visited S.H.A.E.F., Eisenhower had told him that "it would be madness" to deprive the Germans of their natural resources and he rejected all arguments to the contrary. In *Crusade in Europe* Eisenhower bluntly describes his attitude:

"I emphatically repudiated one suggestion I had heard that the Ruhr mines should be flooded. This seemed silly and criminal to me . . . These views were presented to everyone who queried me on the subject, both then and later. They were eventually placed before the President and the Secretary of State when they came to Potsdam in July 1945.''

Harry Hopkins himself joined this protest; Roosevelt and Morgenthau therefore had to shelve indefinitely the plan so accurately described by General Eisenhower. Moreover in London, the Treasury informed the Prime Minister that if German productivity were completely destroyed, she would no longer be able to pay for her imports, and England would therefore lose an important market as soon as peace came. The argument with which Morgenthau had won over Lord Cherwell was therefore entirely refuted. In these circumstances, Churchill made no bones about going back on his agreement, and was quite ready, when he wrote the penultimate volume of his war memoirs, to forget that he had given it, even in writing: he had in fact contributed to drawing up the resolution that had been formulated. The Morgenthau plan was a dead letter.

German propaganda benefits

However, the Morgenthau plan had certain consequences, even though it had been abandoned by the Western Allies. What was learned of it in Germany gave Goebbels a propaganda line which he developed on the radio with his usual diabolical skill. The Allies, he pointed out to his fellow countrymen on every possible occasion, were not only making war against the Nazis, but against the whole German people, who would be condemned to the bleakest poverty by a ruthless enemy if they were so naïve as to cease their resistance and disown their Führer; in destructive purpose, Anglo-Saxon "Jewry" was no different from the Moscow Bolsheviks. The Quebec resolution, moreover, demonstrated the error of people who, like the July 20 conspirators, thought they could spare the German people the Soviet invasion by paying for it at the price of capitulation to the West.

The MOSCOW Conference

''Que diable allait-il faire dans cette galère?'' (What on earth was he doing in his company?) One might well echo Molière's question when considering the visit Churchill made to Moscow from October 9 to 16, 1944.

According to Churchill's own account, the Soviet penetration into south-east Europe compelled him to make this journey. With Rumania's about-face, followed by the Bulgarian armistice, the launching of the Soviet autumn offensive, and "in spite of the Warsaw tragedy . . . I felt the need of another personal meeting with Stalin . . . As the victory of the Grand Alliance became only a matter of time it was natural that Russian ambitions should grow. Communism raised its head behind the thundering Russian battle-front. Russia was the Deliverer, and Communism the gospel she brought.''

At this juncture, neither Bulgaria's nor Rumania's fates were of the slightest concern to Great Britain; on the other hand Churchill was very worried about what would happen to Poland and Greece.

Great Britain considered herself responsible for the restoration of their governments-in-exile, if this was what their peoples really wished. And it was essential that they should be able to express themselves freely. In fact, this was far from certain since Stalin had set up a Polish government subservient to him in Lublin, and George Papandreou's Greek Government seemed to be dependent on the Communist resistance group.

On the other hand, work was not proceeding well at Dumbarton Oaks, where an inter-Allied conference was meeting for the purpose of laying the foundations of a future United Nations Organisation. The Russians clashed with the British and Americans both on the composition of the General Assembly and on the balloting method for the Security Council. Moscow was now determined that the rule of Great Power unanimity should prevail. Once again, according to Churchill in 1953, he felt he should strike while the iron was hot:

"I felt sure we could only reach good

△ *Lord Moran, Churchill's ever-present physician. He saw Churchill every day and was able to note his reaction to events as they happened. His book* Churchill: The Struggle for Survival *thus provides valuable insight into Churchill's thoughts, especially with regard to his attitude towards the Morgenthau Plan and the settlement of the Polish question.*

decisions with Russia while we had the comradeship of a common foe as a bond. Hitler and Hitlerism were doomed; but after Hitler what?"

Churchill's initiative

Therefore Churchill took the initiative in a telegram on September 27, and proposed a visit to the Kremlin. Stalin, in his reply of September 30, welcomed the idea "warmly". Roosevelt excused himself from accompanying Churchill to Moscow as the presidential elections were imminent, and his absence from the U.S.A. at this time might well have prejudiced the result to his disadvantage. However, his ambassador in the U.S.S.R., Averell Harriman, was to replace him, taking part in the conversations as an observer, and as Roosevelt's message of October 4 stated:

"While naturally Averell will not be in a position to commit the United States– I could not permit anyone to commit me in advance–he will be able to keep me informed, and I have told him to return and report to me as soon as the conference is over."

And as he feared that his British partner might indulge in some passing whim, Roosevelt sent word to Stalin on the same day:

"I am sure you understand that in this global war there is literally no question, military or political, in which the United States is not interested. I am firmly convinced that the three of us, and only the three of us, can find the solution of the questions still unresolved. In this sense, while appreciating Mr. Churchill's desire for the meeting, I prefer to regard your forthcoming talks with the Prime Minister as preliminary to a meeting of the three of us which can take place any time after the elections here as far as I am concerned."

Churchill does not mention it in his memoirs, but he took great offence at the President's precaution, according to Lord Moran, who in his capacity as Churchill's doctor saw him every day. But what was more serious, according to Moran, by the end of September "the advance of the Red Army has taken possession of [Churchill's] mind. Once they got into a country, it would not be easy to get them out. Our army in Italy was too weak to keep them in check. He might get his

way with Stalin by other means.

"All might be well if he could wi[n] Stalin's friendship. After all it was stupi[d] of the President to suppose that he wa[s] the only person who could manage Stali[n.] Winston told me that he had found h[e] could talk to Stalin as one human bein[g] to another. Stalin, he was sure, would b[e] sensible. He went on to speak of th[is] proffer of friendship to Stalin as if it wer[e] an ingenious idea that had just occurre[d] to him, and while he spoke his eye[s] popped and his words tumbled over eac[h] other in his excitement. He could think o[f] nothing else. It had ceased to be a mean[s] to an end; it had become an end in itsel[f.] He sat up in bed.

"'If we three come together,' he sai[d] 'everything is possible–absolutely any[-] thing.'"

As can be seen, there is a stron[g] difference between Churchill's attitud[e] in his memoirs and his reactions at th[e] time as his doctor saw them; in 195[3] when the cold war was at its height an[d] he had just been re-elected, Churchi[ll] could not admit to his readers that he ha[d] deluded himself into thinking he coul[d] win Stalin over.

Spheres of influence

Accompanied by Anthony Eden, Genera[l] Sir Hastings Ismay, his chief-of-staff, an[d] Field-Marshal Sir Alan Brooke, th[e] C.I.G.S., the Prime Minister travelled vi[a] Naples, Cairo, and Simferopol' an[d] arrived in Moscow on the evening o[f] October 9. At 2200 hours, he and Ede[n] were conducted to Stalin's office. Stali[n,] accompanied by Molotov, was waitin[g] for him. And in the absence of Averel[l] Harriman, the four men lost no time i[n] making a preliminary survey of th[e] world situation.

Doubtless Harriman would not hav[e] objected to their decision to invite th[e] Polish government to send a delegatio[n] to Moscow. But perhaps he would hav[e] thought that Churchill was unduly com[-] promising the future as well as th[e] U.S.A. if he had heard him tell Stali[n:]

"Let us settle about our affairs in th[e] Balkans. Your armies are in Roumani[a] and Bulgaria. We have interest[s,] missions, and agents there. Don't le[t] us get at cross-purposes in small ways. S[o] far as Britain and Russia are concerned[,] how would it do for you to have ninety[-]

2248

per cent predominance in Roumania, for us to have ninety per cent of the say in Greece, and go fifty-fifty about Yugoslavia?"

And even more so if he had seen Churchill make in writing a proposal which had never been agreed by London and Washington. Churchill in fact, whilst his words were being translated, scribbled on a half sheet of paper:

"Roumania
Russia 90%
The others 10%
Greece
Great Britain 90%
(in accord with U.S.A.)

△ △ The "Red Orchestra" batters Nazi ears with its successes in Poland and East Prussia.
△ ◁ How Simplicissimus saw "free" Polish broadcasts from the "Soviet paradise".
△ John Bull tells Poland "The best solution is to give him all he steals and you'll be friends."

△ *George Papandreou, Greek Prime Minister. In April 1944, he was brought out of Greece by the Allies to form a Greek government-in-exile in Cairo. Churchill was concerned about the fate of Greece after the war and considered Great Britain responsible for the restoration of the government-in-exile. When the Germans withdrew from Greece in October 1944, Papandreou returned to Athens as Prime Minister.*

▷ *Churchill arrives in Moscow, October 9, 1944. Concerned by the increasing Soviet penetration of south-east Europe, Churchill initiated this conference himself, determined to reach amicable agreement with Stalin over the future of the Balkans and, more important, Poland.*

Russia	..	..	..	10%
Yugoslavia	..	..	50-50%
Hungary	..	..	50-50%
Bulgaria			
Russia	..	..	..	75%
The others	..	..	25%"

Stalin ticked the paper passed to him by Churchill, who writes: "It was all settled in no more time than it takes to set down."

In his memoirs, Churchill assures us it was only valid for the duration of the war and that it did not prejudice solution which would be kept for the future pea conference. But if we accept this versio it is hard to understand the irritatic with which he writes a few lines late

"'Might it not be thought rathe cynical if it seemed we had disposed these issues, so fateful to millions people, in such an offhand manner Let us burn the paper.' 'No, you keep it said Stalin."

In exchange for a half-sheet of pape

e Western Powers, on Churchill's initiave, had abdicated all influence in Buchast and Sofia, and implicitly left the umanians and Bulgarians to face the oviet giant alone.

In addition, it was later observed that is arrangement on October 9 did not move the threat of Communist subrsion from Greece, in spite of the perntage of that unhappy country conded to Great Britain by the Kremlin.

ito goes it alone

e 50 per cent influence allotted to ritain in Yugoslavia dropped to zero en before hostilities ended in Europe, d Tito tore up the agreement he had ncluded in the previous year with Dr. ubašić, Prime Minister of the Yugoav government-in-exile. Obviously, in ctober 1944, Churchill and Eden no nger had any illusions about the future rection of Marshal Tito's policy, in ite of the Anglo-American arms deveries which had saved him from defeat d death. Moreover, in this division of heres of influence, it was clear that hurchill had completely forgotten Alania, on which Greece had some claims.

den *versus* Molotov

ut before 24 hours had passed, Molotov ied to obtain from Eden some modificaons of the percentages agreed on the y before. He received a curt refusal, ut a note of Eden's shows that his own port of the incident was coolly received y the Prime Minister, who was wrapped p in his own illusions:

"W. rather upset by my report. I think e thought I had dispelled good atmoshere he had created night before. But I xplained this was the real battle and I ould not and would not give way."

His firmness was rewarded, as Molotov ndertook to call on the Bulgarians to vacuate immediately the Greek and ugoslav provinces which they had ccupied by German agreement in April nd May 1941. As regards Yugoslavia, den wrote:

"We also spoke of Yugoslavia, when talin said that Tito thought the Croats nd Slovenes would refuse to join in any overnment under King Peter. He himself had the impression that the King was ineffective. I replied that I was sure the King had courage and I thought that he had intelligence. Mr. Churchill interjected that the King was very young.

"'How old is he?' asked Stalin. 'Twenty-one,' I answered. 'Twenty-one!' exclaimed Stalin with a burst of pride, 'Peter the Great was ruler of Russia at seventeen.' For that moment, at least, Stalin was more nationalist than communist, the same mood as had seen the disappearance for the time being of the portraits of Marx and Engels from the Kremlin rooms and their replacement by Kutuzov and Suvorov."

Poles in exile

On October 13, the Polish delegation of the government-in-exile, consisting of its Prime Minister, Stanislas Mikolajczyk, Professor Grabski, and Foreign Minister Tadeusz Romer started discussions with Stalin, Molotov, Churchill, Eden, and Harriman, who had been instructed to keep strictly to his rôle as observer. They intended to reach an agreement on two questions: firstly, the eastern frontiers of Poland; and secondly, the formation of a unified Polish government, including the London government's representatives and members of the Lublin "National Committee". Although they expected to make some territorial sacrifices to the Soviet Union, Mikolajczyk and his colleagues were aghast when they discovered that the Teheran agreement (which had been concluded behind their backs by the "Big Three") had prescribed the Curzon Line as their country's frontier; thus 48 per cent of Polish territory would be surrendered to the U.S.S.R. without the population involved being consulted about the transfer.

The Polish prime minister's protests against the acquiescence which was being demanded of him left Stalin cold and uncompromising.

After this session, the British and Poles met. Churchill lost his temper and started threatening the unfortunate Mikolajczyk:

"I pressed Mikolajczyk hard to consider two things, namely, *de facto* acceptance of the Curzon Line, with interchange of population, and a friendly discussion with the Lublin Polish Committee so that a united Poland might be established."

△ *Averell Harriman* (right), *U.S. Ambassador in Moscow, with Anthony Eden, who accompanied Churchill to the Moscow Conference. Harriman represented Roosevelt at the conference, but was absent when Stalin and Churchill decided on spheres of influence in the Balkans.*

BALANCE OF POWER

This is the version of the meeting in Churchill's memoirs, but it seems to be a typically British understatement. In fact, on the next day the Prime Minister confided to Moran: "I was pretty rough with Mikolajczyk . . . He was obstinate and I lost my temper." A few hours later Churchill returned to the subject: "I shook my fist at him and lost my temper."

It is hard to accept Mikolajczyk's account of the conversation; his memoirs were published in New York and Toronto and were not challenged by Churchill. The striking thing about Churchill's diatribes, as recounted by Mikolajczyk, is not so much their violence ("You're not a government! You're an unreasonable people who want to shipwreck Europe. I'll leave you to stew in your own juice. You have no sense of responsibility when you want to abandon the people in your care, and you've no idea of their sufferings. You've no thought for anything but your own wretched, mean, and egotistical interests.") and their threats ("We shall not part as friends. I shall tell the world how unreasonable you've shown yourselves to be . . . We'll take a stand and break away from you if you continue to prevaricate. I'll consider opening relations with the other Poles. The Lublin government can work perfectly. They'll be the government for sure.") as his confidence that if the Polish Government gave in to the Big Three, all would be for the best in the best of all possible Europes. Churchill continued:

"Our relations with Russia are better than they've ever been. I expect them to remain so . . . we do not intend to jeopardise the peace of Europe . . . Your discussions are nothing more than criminal attempts to undermine goodwill between the Allies with your *Liberum veto*. It is a criminal act of your doing!"

Assuming this determinedly optimistic point of view, Churchill described to Mikolajczyk the advantage which would compensate Poland for the sacrifices he was calling upon her to make:

"But think what you will get in exchange. You will have a country. I will see that a British ambassador is sent to you. And there will also be an ambassador from the United States, the greatest military power in the world . . .

"If you accept the Curzon line, the United States will devote themselves most actively to the reconstruction of Poland and will doubtless give you large loans, perhaps even without your having to ask

for them. We will help you too, but we will be poor after this war. You are *obliged* to accept the decision of the great powers."

Mikolajczyk, in spite of Churchill's tone of voice, was not completely insensitive to this argument. He proposed a compromise, in which he was prepared to recognise the Curzon Line as Poland's eastern frontier, provided that the Drohobycz and Boryslaw oil wells, as well as the great historically and traditionally Polish cities of L'vov and Vilnyus on the east of the line, remained Polish. But Stalin refused to countenance any such concessions.

Combined Polish government?

In doing this, Stalin was risking nothing; on the one hand his armies had crossed the Curzon Line on the entire front between the Niemen and the Carpathians; on the other hand, the Lublin Committee delegates, Osóbka-Morawski and Bierut, stated in the presence of Churchill, Eden, and Harriman:

"'We are here to demand on behalf of Poland that Lvov shall belong to Russia. That is the will of the Polish people.'

"When this had been translated from Polish into English and Russian I looked at Stalin and saw an understanding twinkle in his expressive eyes, as much as to say, 'What about that for our Soviet teaching!'"

In their memoirs Churchill and Eden made no attempt to conceal their disgust when they heard these servile commonplaces. Nevertheless Mikolajczyk received the peremptory advice to accept these foreign agents in his government. Otherwise it would be the end of Poland.

Conduct of the war

As Roosevelt had wished, the problems relating to the articles of the future international organisation were not mentioned during the conference. The agenda was devoted to presenting, discussing, and putting final touches to the plans for the last phase of the war in Europe and for the participation of the Red Army in the war against Japan.

△ *Marshal Josep Broz "Tito", Yugoslav Communist Party chief and leader of the partisan resistance movement. Tito won British support and aid in 1943, and by August 1944 the Germans were retreating before the partisans. The future of Yugoslavia was discussed at Moscow, but Tito refused to countenance the restoration of King Peter. In March 1945, he set up a provisional government with himself as Prime Minister.*
△ ◁ ◁ *"And look! The nice uncle is even offering you a stool."*
△ ◁ *The imbalance of power by late on in the war.*
▽ ◁ *Poland's pathetic plight: "And we all put our faith in this boat."*

With his usual clarity, Brooke set out the situation on the Western Front and in Italy, and explained General Eisenhower's intentions. The deputy chief-of-staff of the Red Army, General Antonov, then spoke, and Brooke noted in his diary that he was extremely pleased with the ensuing discussion.

On October 15, the war against Japan was discussed, with particular reference to the Red Army and the possibility of moving supplies via the trans-Siberian railway for an offensive in Manchuria with 60 divisions and appropriate air forces. Stalin took over from his military colleague and explained the difficulties of the project. According to Brooke:

"He displayed an astounding knowledge of technical railway details, had read past history of fighting in that theatre and from this knowledge drew very sound deductions. I was more than ever impressed by his military ability."

Violate Swiss neutrality?

Complete military agreement was reached by the Big Three; Stalin, however, made one suggestion that was rejected by Churchill, although he does not mention it in his memoirs. On the other hand, Admiral Leahy wrote:

"Harriman reported on October 13 that Stalin advocated only a holding effort in North Italy, coupled with an advance toward Vienna from the head of the Adriatic Sea. The Soviet chieftain also advocated an advance through Switzerland to get into the rear of the Siegfried Line fortifications. The latter suggestion certainly did not place much value on the Allied claim that the sovereignty of small states must not be violated."

In June 1966, Harriman's despatch concerning this suggestion was published by the State Department, together with the diplomatic documents of the time. We can therefore make the following correction to Leahy's statement. Stalin did not advise his Western Allies to pursue their attack in northern Italy but, noting that the Germans were resisting them strongly in the Apennines and on the Siegfried Line, he suggested that they should withdraw ten of the 25 divisions which were in the line between the Adriatic and the Tyrrhenian Sea. These divisions would invade Switzerland, turn

△ Bierut, President of the Lublin "Committee of National Liberation". Churchill thought the Lublin Poles were "mere pawns of Russia" when he met them at the Moscow Conference.
▷ The Communist provisional government of Poland at a march-past in Lublin. The officers are saluting in the traditional Polish manner, with three fingers (one for the Father, one for the Son, and one for the Holy Ghost) despite their new Communist persuasion.
△▷ Roosevelt, on board the cruiser Quincy travelling to the Yalta Conference, stops off in the Great Bitter Lakes to entertain King Farouk of Egypt on his birthday. This delighted Farouk, who had felt slighted by other Allied leaders.
▽▷ London, Washington, and Moscow recognised General de Gaulle's provisional government as the government of the French Republic at the Moscow Conference. Here, General de Gaulle is seen arriving at Moscow. He was not, however, invited to the Yalta and Potsdam Conferences.

the German defences north of Basle and attempt to co-ordinate its operations with the Red Army's in Austria. Switzerland, he stated, had played a double game during the war and must be compelled by force of arms to give the Allies access to her territory.

Churchill, according to Harriman's report, opposed this plan energetically, not only because it was militarily impracticable, which was true, but even more because it was contrary to the Western Allies' political principles. Stalin did not persist with the idea. Churchill, however, was so impressed by the bitterly hostile way Stalin spoke about Switzerland that on December 3 he dictated the following note to Eden:

"I put this down for record. Of all the neutrals Switzerland has the greatest right to distinction. She has been the sole international force linking the hideously sundered nations and ourselves. What does it matter whether she has been able to give us the commercial advantages we desire or has given too many to the Germans, to keep herself alive? She has been a democratic State, standing for freedom in self-defence among her mountains, and in thought, in spite of race, largely on our side.

"I was astonished at U.J.'s [Uncle Joe

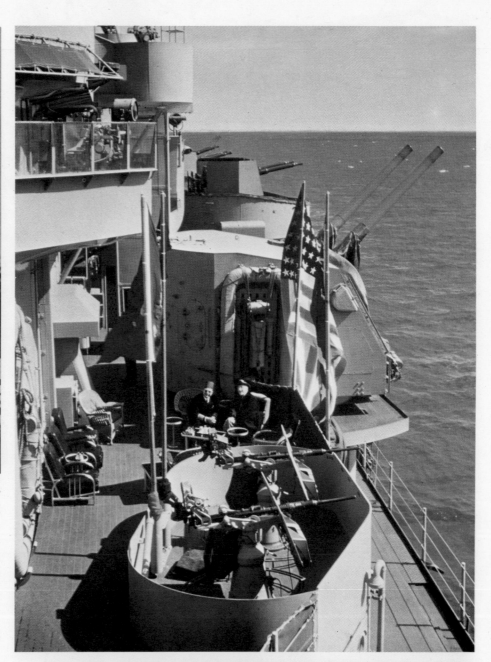

Churchill's and Roosevelt's name for [Stalin] savageness against her, and, much though I respect that great and good man, I was entirely uninfluenced by his attitude. He called them 'swine', and does not use that sort of language without meaning it. I am sure we ought to stand by Switzerland, and we ought to explain to U.J. why it is we do so. The moment for sending such a message should be carefully chosen . . ."

He also, via secret channels, alerted the Swiss Federal Council, which received the warning gratefully.

Germany to be divided

Churchill and Stalin decided that Germany would be divided up and that a southern state, consisting of Baden, Württemberg, Bavaria, and Austria, should be formed. To give more stability to this Danubian confederation, Churchill wanted Hungary to join it, but Stalin, who had designs on Hungary, refused. The only success claimed by the British government was the *de jure* recognition by London, Washington, and Moscow of General de Gaulle's provisional government as the government of France.

The YALTA Conference

[M]uch has been written, at any rate in the [W]est, about the "Argonaut" Conference, [d]uring which Roosevelt, Churchill, [St]alin, and their chief political and [m]ilitary colleagues met at Yalta in the [C]rimea. In 1955, the State Department [pu]blished a wide collection of diplomatic [d]ocuments relating to the Big Three's [m]eeting, the discussions they had to-[g]ether, and the resolutions and agree-[m]ents they signed. Thus we can compare [th]ese authentic records with the state-[m]ents of those taking part in the con-[fe]rence.

During the period between Churchill's [M]oscow journey and the Yalta con-[fe]rence, a number of occurrences which [in]fluenced the course of negotiations [sh]ould be mentioned.

On November 7, 1944, the American [pe]ople re-elected Roosevelt to a fourth [te]rm as President, admittedly by about [3,0]00,000 fewer votes than in 1940. Ob-[vi]ously, in making his choice, the [A]merican voter was relying on the adage [th]at one should not change horses in

mid-course. Nevertheless, the victor of this exhausting campaign had neglected his brief and, in addition, he was in a very poor state of health.

"The President looked old and thin and drawn; he had a cape or shawl over his shoulders and appeared shrunken; he sat looking straight ahead with his mouth open, as if he were not taking things in." This was Moran's description of him on February 3, and the next day he wrote:

"It was not only his physical deteriora-tion that had caught their attention. He intervened very little in the discussions, sitting with his mouth open. If he has sometimes been short of facts about the subject under discussion his shrewdness has covered this up. Now, they say, the shrewdness has gone, and there is nothing left." Again, Moran noted on the 7th:

"To a doctor's eye, the President appears a very sick man. He has all the symptoms of hardening of the arteries of the brain in an advanced stage, so that I give him only a few months to live."

For personal reasons Roosevelt, before

◄ *The splendid Livadia Palace, where the Yalta Conference was held to decide the fate of the world.*

Molotov signs the Franco-Russian pact, watched by de Gaulle and Stalin. But by the time of the Yalta Conference relations were not so amicable.

starting on his electoral campaign, had dropped his previous Vice-President, Henry A. Wallace, in favour of Harry S. Truman, the senator from Missouri. This was a stroke of luck for the free world. Truman, a man of strong character, was, however, quite unprepared for his task when on April 12, 1945 he was suddenly called upon to take over the responsibilities of power.

Moreover the Secretary of State, Cordell Hull, had now reached retirement age. Roosevelt appointed Edward R. Stettinius in his place. Stettinius was a conscientious civil servant who knew his job thoroughly, but he was called upon to take over his duties under a President in very poor health, to say the least, and was faced by an opposite number as redoubtable and experienced in international affairs as Molotov.

Stalin recognises the "Lublin Committee"

Mikolajczyk, when he returned to London, found that the majority of his government disapproved of the concessions he had felt compelled to make to the U.S.S.R. He therefore accepted the consequences, and resigned. He was succeeded by Tomasz Arciszewski, a militant social-democrat. But although he was more to the left than his predecessor, the new head of the exile government failed to move the Kremlin.

When he resigned on November 24, 1944, Mikolajczyk handed over two documents concerning the policy of the U.S.A. and Great Britain towards the future Polish state. In a letter after he had been re-elected, President Roosevelt defined the American attitude clearly and positively:

"The Government of the United States is, most determinedly, in favour of a strong Polish state, free, independent, and conscious of the rights of the Polish people, to run its internal politics as it sees fit, without any outside interference."

Certainly the U.S.A. could not depart from their traditional policy and guarantee the frontiers of the future Polish state, but they were ready to play a very large part in its economic reconstruction.

Moreover, on the previous November 2, on Churchill's instructions, Sir Alexander Cadogan, Permanent Under-Secretary

of State at the Foreign Office, wrote Romer, the Polish Foreign Minister, letter of which the following is an extrac

"Finally you ask if His Majesty Government will guarantee the indepe dence and integrity of the new Poli state. On this point the reply of H Majesty's Government is that they a ready to give this guarantee conjoint with the Soviet Government. If t Government of the United States al believed that it could associate itse in this guarantee, that would be so muc the better, but His Majesty's Governme does not make this a condition of t guarantee, which it is ready to give co jointly with that of the Soviet Gover ment."

It is evident that Great Britain's attitu in this declaration fell considerably sho of the U.S.A.'s, as she made her guarant of Polish independence subject to ε agreement with the Soviet Union. Wh would happen if Stalin refused th guarantee?

On December 18, a statement Secretary of State Stettinius, recallir the terms of Roosevelt's letter to Mik lajczyk, was brought to Stalin's notice. C December 27, Stalin in his reply to Roos velt maintained that this statement ha been overtaken by events; then after long diatribe against Arciszewski and h colleagues, he added in so many word

"I must say frankly that in the eve of the Polish Committee of Nation Liberation becoming a Provisional Poli Government, the Soviet Government wi in view of the foregoing, have no seriou reasons for postponing its recognition

Then, in spite of a letter from Roosevel who said he was "disturbed and deep disappointed" by this declaration and the hasty Moscow decision, he proceede to recognise the Lublin Committee January 5, 1945; he gave Roosevelt th following explanation:

"Of course I quite understand yo proposal for postponing recognition of th Provisional Government of Poland by th Soviet Union for a month. But one circun stance makes me powerless to compl with your wish. The point is that o December 27 the Presidium of the Suprem Soviet of the U.S.S.R., replying to th corresponding question by the Pole declared that it would recognise th Provisional Government of Poland th moment it was set up. This circumstanc makes me powerless to comply with you wish."

But he omitted to say that he had dictated this request for recognition to the "Polish Committee of National Liberation."

The new government moves in

It was in this sort of atmosphere that the Yalta Conference opened. Certainly Roosevelt had no intention of recognising the puppet government which Stalin controlled, and Churchill even less so. But in the meantime events had moved on. In fact just when the three delegations were holding their first session, Zhukov's advance guard reached the bend of the Oder whilst Konev's was about to take Breslau. Except for the Polish corridor, all Polish territory was in the hands of the Russians, who were everywhere setting up the Lublin Committee's representatives and hunting down the partisans who had been fighting the Germans for five years under the command of the Polish government-in-exile.

The conference opens

On February 2, Roosevelt, who had arrived on the cruiser *Quincy,* and Churchill, who had flown in, met at Valletta in Malta. They joined the Combined Chiefs-of-Staff Committee, which had been in session for three days and was completing plans for the great operation to take the British and the Americans into the centre of Germany. Then the two delegations flew to the Crimea and on the evening of February 3 moved into the buildings reserved for them: the Americans into the former imperial palace of Livadia; the British five miles away in

1. *Harry Hopkins*
2. *Alger Hiss*
3. *James V. Forrestal*
4. *Robert Winant*
5. *Edward R. Stettinius*

the Vorontzov villa. Stalin and his colleagues were to stay at the Yusupov Palace halfway between them, an arrangement obviously calculated to prevent any Anglo-American private conversations and to make *tête-à-tête* talks with Roosevelt easier.

The first such meeting took place in the afternoon of February 4, and the President was moved to get Stalin to repeat his Teheran toast (that 50,000 German officers should be shot) because Roosevelt maintained the devastation caused by the Wehrmacht in the Crimea gave him a desire for revenge.

Roosevelt chosen as chairman

A few hours later the conference opene in the Livadia Palace, and Stalin im mediately proposed that there should k no rotation of chairmanship, but tha Roosevelt should chair the proceeding for the whole meeting.

Arthur Conte, in his *Yalta ou le parta du monde*, has noted that this was a skilf Soviet manoeuvre, as it was not intende

American vacillation

Eden also noted that the American president was "vague and loose and ineffective", letting the discussion drift on, without being able to pin Stalin and Churchill down to firm and precise terms. The various questions on the agenda were discussed unmethodically, by fits and starts, and Harry Hopkins several times had to bring the discussion back to the subject by passing notes to Roosevelt. But the bias of these notes can easily be guessed, as in spite of the troublesome state of his health, the so-called *éminence grise* of the White House was still strongly pro-Soviet.

Secretary of State Stettinius was too new in his job to know how to assert himself usefully in the discussion. As for the fourth member of the American delegation, the diplomat Alger Hiss, whose particular responsibility was questions relating to the future United Nations Organisation, he was later condemned to five years' imprisonment on January 22, 1950 by a New York court for perjury about his Communist associations.

Another circumstance played against the two Western powers; this was the ten day period allowed by the American constitution to the President to approve or veto bills adopted by the Congress. As he could not do this by cable or radio, it was essential for him not to prolong his stay in the Crimea beyond a week. Stalin, however, was in no hurry and was ready to sell Roosevelt time in exchange for concessions.

△ ◁ *The Combined Chiefs-of-Staff Committee in session in Malta, January-February 1944, completing plans for the advance into central Germany. Roosevelt and Churchill joined the committee briefly before continuing their journey to Yalta.*
▽ ◁ ◁ *Reunion on board the cruiser* Quincy, *at anchor off Malta: Roosevelt, General Marshall (on the right), Vice-Admiral Cooke (on the left), and Admiral King (back view).*
▽ ◁ *Churchill and Roosevelt acknowledge their reception at Yalta. Molotov is on Churchill's right. Note how ill Roosevelt looks; Lord Moran said at the time that he appeared "shrunken".*
△ *Russia sits down to a nourishing bowl of "little states of Europe" soup, with the comment "You can see how happy I am to swallow up the people you abandoned and I freed." In the pot in this German cartoon are Lithuania, Finland, and Holland.*

Formidable negotiator

erely as a practical working arrangement: "This also showed a remarkable appreciation of Roosevelt's psychology, strengthening him in the awareness his superiority. He was also dissociating mself from British imperialism. It in ct separated the British and the Americans by conferring the chairmanship the American; Roosevelt thus had wer to arbitrate, a conciliatory rôle hich would naturally lead him to show creased understanding of the Russian osition. Stalin immediately gave himlf a big advantage while appearing to ve it to Roosevelt."

Since he had seen Stalin at work, Anthony Eden refers to his diplomatic talents in a way that reminds one of Field-Marshal Sir Alan Brooke's references to his strategic abilities:

"Marshal Stalin as a negotiator was the toughest proposition of all. Indeed, after something like thirty years' experience of international conferences of one kind and another, if I had to pick a team for going into a conference room, Stalin would be my first choice. Of course the man was ruthless and of course he knew his purpose. He never wasted a word. He never stormed, he was

Three German comments on Allied relations:

△ *Stalin, past master of the shot-in-the-neck method of execution, sets the table for the next conference with his latest invention.*

△▷ *"I have the feeling, my dear Roosevelt, that we've been left decidedly behind the marshal," says Churchill.*

▷ *Overheard during the post-war carve-up of the world: "Well, Sam, what are you doing?" "I was just thinking how I could repay you for your great help." "Incredible! I was just thinking the same thing."*

another gratefully: "After the rain com the sun."

seldom even irritated. Hooded, calm, never raising his voice, he avoided the repeated negatives of Molotov which were so exasperating to listen to. By more subtle methods he got what he wanted without having seemed so obdurate."

Nevertheless, Eden also acknowledged that Molotov was a first-rate assistant to Stalin. One may well suppose that when responsibilities were assigned, the orders given to Molotov were to adopt such a harsh tone that when Stalin took over negotiations in the style so vividly described by Eden, the British and American representatives (in particular Roosevelt, Stettinius, and James) could tell one

Churchill's difficult positio

Under these circumstances it is not ha to see that the British delegation had easy task, faced with the vacillations American policy and Stalin's firm resol to make the maximum possible advance in all parts of the world. Thus the Britis did not receive the immediate suppo of their natural allies when they propose the immediate and simultaneous evacu tion of Persia by the British and Sovi forces that had occupied the countr since August 1941. Similarly, the Sovi Union succeeded in imposing its attitu about a revision, once peace came, of th

◁ *The three delegations get down to work. Stalin is seated second from left at the top, Roosevelt at the right, and Churchill at bottom left, with a cigar.*

△ *Death comments "But why argue about future supplies of cannon fodder, my dear sirs? I'm quite content with your present ones."*

▽ ◁ *Eden comments on his Russian opposite number: "Molotov clearly isn't a devious character. His territorial ambitions aren't difficult to see."*

Montreux Convention. This had, since July 20, 1936, laid down the law concerning the control of the Turkish narrows. Russia was thus in a position to start a very unpleasant quarrel with Turkey until President Truman intervened and restored order.

Therefore Churchill left the Crimea full of forebodings, quite the reverse of his happy mood of the previous October 9, when he landed at Moscow airport. But to the last day of his life he did his best to deny any responsibility for the inexorable process which led to the enslavement of 120 million Europeans behind the Iron Curtain. According to Churchill, everything was decided at Yalta during the conference when he was, if one can put it like that, "sandwiched" between Stalin and Roosevelt. In this way he was able to divest himself of his responsibility

in this most unjust settlement of World War II, making Roosevelt shoulder it all. But in view of the documents just quoted, it is impossible to confirm this black and white judgement, and Alfred Fabre-Luce's judgement in *L'Histoire démaquillée,*

△ *Stalin and Roosevelt. The latter, now a very sick man, unwittingly allowed himself to be used as Stalin's pawn in destroying the strength of the Western alliance.*

"Churchill changed tack too late", seems more correct. All the same, he changed tack a year before Truman.

The resolutions

We may now quote the resolutions adopted by Churchill, Roosevelt, and Stalin and drawn up by Eden, Stettinius, and Molotov. We shall limit our comments to the resolutions on Poland, Germany, and the Far East.

(a) The reorganisation of Poland

Stalin conceded to the Allies that the Soviet-Polish frontier could in places run three and even five miles to the east of the Curzon Line, which he claimed had been originated by Clemenceau, although neither the British nor the Americans pointed out this obvious historical error. The Oder and the Neisse were to constitute the western frontier of the new Poland. But although, at Teheran, they had agreed on the eastern Neisse (which runs through the town of Neisse), as is clear from a question from Churchill concerning the allocation of the upper Silesian industrial basin, Stalin and Molotov claimed they had been referring to the western Neisse, which meets the Oder between Guben and Fürstenberg.

Churchill pointed out in vain that thi additional modification of the Germa Polish frontier would entail the furthe expulsion of eight million Germans. Stali replied that the matter was now settlec as the province's inhabitants had fle from the Soviet advance, which was onl half true, and they then went on to co sider the agenda.

As regards Poland's politic reorganisation, we must refer to Point of the protocol recorded on February 1 by the foreign ministers of the Big Three Taking into consideration the Red Army complete "liberation" of Poland, it statec

"The provisional government actuall operating in Poland must in the futur be reorganised on a larger democrati base, to include the popular leader actually in Poland and those abroac This new government is to be called th Polish Government of National Unity

"Mr. Molotov, Mr. Harriman, and S A. Clark Kerr are authorised to form commission to consult initially the men bers of the Provisional Polish Goverr ment, as well as other Polish leaders (bot in Poland and abroad), with a view to th reorganisation of the actual governmen along the lines set out below. The Polis Government of National Unity must se about organising free and open election as soon as possible, on the basis of a univer

The Partition of Poland

- —— Polish boundary in 1937
- —— Polish boundary in 1947
- —— Curzon Line

Niemen

Vilnyus

Gdynia
Danzig

EAST PRUSSIA

U.S.S.R.

Wolin

Stettin

Oder

Toruń

Vistula

Bug

GERMANY

Frankfurt

Warsaw

Brest-Litovsk

POLAND

Görlitz

Breslau

Kraków

L'vov

Drohobycz

Stanislaw

CZECHOSLOVAKIA

HUNGARY

RUMANIA

Anthony Eden, the British Foreign Secretary at the time of the Yalta Conference, was born in 1897 and served on the Western Front in World War I. He was Minister for League of Nations Affairs in 1933 and took over from Sir Samuel Hoare as Foreign Secretary in December. He resigned as a result of the weak British attitude to Italy in 1938. Eden became Dominions Secretary, Secretary of State for War, and finally Foreign Secretary in Churchill's Coalition Government in the War. He proved himself a very able diplomat with a flair for persuasion.

al franchise and a secret ballot. All emocratic and anti-Nazi parties will ave the right to take part and put up andidates."

It can be seen that there is a great ifference between this tripartite declaraion and Stalin's statement to Roosevelt n May 4, 1943: "As regards the Hitlerites' umours on the possibility that a new Polish government will be formed in the J.S.S.R., it is scarcely necessary to give he lie to these ravings."

The two Western powers did not xpressly recognise the government forned from the Lublin Committee, but they ook note of its existence, and the men ⁓ho were to give it the character of ational unity provided for by the protocol athered round it and not round the legal overnment in London. No one stated ow many of these men were to come from ondon and how many from Lublin; ut this question was to be examined by a ommission and Molotov, who was to be

at its centre, would have much greater authority than the British and American Ambassadors in Moscow.

(b) Germany's fate

In order to snatch these concessions from his allies, in exchange for a more vague promise of "free and open elections on the basis of a universal franchise and a secret ballot", Stalin put forward the argument that in the event of a German revival the Soviet Union's security demanded the existence of an independent and friendly Poland. In this respect, it is odd to note that neither Churchill nor Roosevelt thought of pointing out to Stalin that the arrangements they had just decided on for the treatment of Germany eliminated any danger of aggression on her part for centuries to come.

Apart from the Oder-Neisse frontier which was to be imposed on Germany, Point 3 of the Yalta protocol is absolutely clear in this respect. Churchill and Eden with some difficulty secured France's

△ *The post-war settlement of Poland agreed at Yalta. In effect the country was shifted to the west, losing her eastern areas but gaining new western ones from Germany.*

△ *Warsaw after the Rising: in the course of the fighting the city was almost completely destroyed, and afterwards the Germans moved in forced labour and tidied the ruins into great piles of bricks.*

right to take part in the occupation of Germany and to send delegates to sit on the Allied Control Commission charged with administering the defeated power. In spite of the treaty he had just signed with General de Gaulle, Stalin at first refused this in terms that were most offensive to France.

As for Roosevelt, he wavered between these two opposing points of view and finally sided with Churchill; but it was agreed that the French occupation zone would be cut out of the British and American zones. It was at this point in the discussions that Roosevelt, in reply to one of Stalin's questions, made a blunder by telling him that he could not possibly obtain authorisation from Congress to maintain American troops in Europe for more than two years after the end of the war. Stalin, it can readily be imagined, found this statement most helpful to his cause.

It was agreed between Roosevelt and Stalin that Germany should pay 20,000 million dollars in reparations; half of this sum would go to the Soviet Union, which would be paid in kind in the form of a transfer of industrial equipment, annual goods deliveries, and the use of German manpower. The final settlement of reparations owed by Germany, and their

distribution among the nations tha suffered as a result of her aggressio would be determined by a commissio in Moscow. Great Britain had reserve her position on the question of the figur of 20,000 million dollars agreed by th Soviets and the Americans.

The principle of dividing Germany u was recorded in the protocol of Februar 11, and was not clarified during the Yalt discussions; the commission set up unde Eden's chairmanship to examine th problem received no directives from th Big Three. It has been assumed from thi silence that it was Stalin's intention t transform the Soviet occupation zon into a Communist state which would b Moscow's satellite. Undoubtedly there i much evidence for this assumption.

(c) The Far East

As Russia's relations with Japan wer governed by the non-aggression pac signed in Moscow on April 13, 1941, th question of Russia taking part in the wa being waged by the Anglo-American against the Japanese was settled by special protocol which was kept secre

As a reward for its intervention, th U.S.S.R. was to recover the rights it ha lost by the Treaty of Portsmouth (U.S.A in 1905 which had crowned the Empero Meiji's victory over Tsar Nichola

As a consequence, it was to regain possession of the southern part of Sakhalin island, the Manchuria railway, the port of Dairen (Lü-ta) which was to be internationalised, and its lease of Port Arthur. In addition, the Russians would receive the Kurile islands, which they had surrendered to Japan in 1875 in exchange for the southern part of Sakhalin island. It is clear that the agreement of February 11, 1945 took little account of the interests of the fourth great power, Chiang Kai-shek's China. Admittedly it was agreed that the eastern China and southern Manchuria railways would be run jointly by a Soviet-Chinese company and that China would retain "full and complete sovereignty" in Manchuria. Nevertheless the power mainly involved in this arrangement had taken no part in the negotiations, and had not even been consulted. On this matter, the agreement merely stated:

It is agreed that the arrangements for Outer Mongolia, as well as for the ports and railways mentioned will require the consent of Generalissimo Chiang Kai-shek. The President will take the necessary measures to obtain this assent, acting on the advice of Marshal Stalin."

But the agreement did not state what would happen if the Chunking government refused its agreement. Moreover, the British and American negotiations about this arrangement lost sight of the fact that as in 1898, the Russian reoccupation of Port Arthur and Dairen in the Kuantung peninsula automatically raised the question of Korea. However, Korea does not appear in the text.

President Roosevelt relied on his own intuition, and did not heed the warnings of Ambassador William Bullitt: "Bill, I am not challenging your facts; they are correct. I am not challenging the logic of your argument. But I have the feeling that Stalin isn't that kind of man. Harry [Hopkins] says he isn't and that all he wants is his country's security. And I think that if I give him all I can give him, and ask for nothing in return, *noblesse oblige*, he won't try to annex anything and he will agree to work with me for a world of democracy and peace."

△ *But in Germany too the rubble was piling up, the result of ever more efficient Allied bombing.* Overleaf: *The harrowing sight that greeted the Allies as they advanced into Germany—the pitiable survivors of the concentration camps.*

CHAPTER 145

Himmler's offensive

fore he could accept the German rrender, the offer of which was to be ought to him at Rheims by a delegation aded by Colonel-General Jodl, General senhower still had to repel two attacks, e directed against his own authority, d the other against the 6th Army Group lower Alsace.

On December 28, 1944, Eisenhower nt to Hasselt, where Montgomery d set up his headquarters. He wanted go over the plans for future operations th him, to begin as soon as the Ardennes cket had been nipped off. Eisen- wer and Montgomery had no difficulty reaching agreement on the objective be set for the offensive they were about to launch. Both favoured the Ruhr. But Montgomery thought that the "major crisis" that had just been resolved autho- rised him to adopt the claim he had pressed at the beginning of the pre- ceding August. He wanted control of operations, and he thought himself the more qualified to bear the responsibility since Eisenhower had put the American 1st and 9th Armies under his command. Hence his letter to "Ike", dated December 29. Point 6 of this read:

"I suggest that your directive should finish with this sentence:

"'12 and 21 Army Groups will develop operations in accordance with the above instructions.

△ *General Leclerc (wearing the* képi) *inspects the men and the machines of his French 2nd Armoured Division. After helping in the defence of Strasbourg during Operation* "Nordwind", *the division was moved south as part of the French II Corps for the crushing of the Colmar pocket.*

"'From now onwards full operational direction, control, and co-ordination of these operations is vested in the C.-in-C. 21 Army Group, subject to such instructions as may be issued by the Supreme Commander from time to time.'"

In writing this, Montgomery was disregarding the prudent advice contained in Brooke's letter of December 24 to him:

"I would like to give you a word of warning. Events and enemy action have forced on Eisenhower the setting up of a more satisfactory system of command. I feel it is most important that you should not even in the slightest degree appear to rub this undoubted fact in to anyone at S.H.A.E.F. or elsewhere."

Eisenhower rejected his subordinate's suggestion by return of post. But, even had he not done this on his own initiative, he would have been ordered to do so by General Marshall, who cabled him from Washington on December 30:

"They may or may not have brought to your attention articles in certain London papers proposing a British deputy commander for all your ground forces and implying that you have undertaken too much of a task yourself. My feeling is this: under no circumstances make any concessions of any kind whatsoever. I am not assuming that you had in mind such a concession I just wish you to be certain of our attitude. You are doing a grand job, and go on and give them hell."

The matter would have stopped there if, on January 5, 1945, Montgomery had not given a press conference on the Battle of the Ardennes, which drove the American generals to the limit of exasperation. The text of the conference was published by General Bradley and it can be said that although Montgomery polished his own image and took some pleasure in exaggerating the part played by British forces in the Ardennes, he did not criticise his allies or their leaders in any way. But the journalists accredited to S.H.A.E.F. and army group seized on his speech and commented bitterly on it, some standing up for Montgomery, others for Eisenhower.

The crisis reached flashpoint when Bradley informed his old friend Eisenhower that he would ask to be recalled to the United States rather than serve under Montgomery's command. In view of the rumours spread by Goebbels's propaganda services, Churchill thought he ought to step in, which he did in the House of Commons on January 18. His excellent

speech made special mention of the important part that the U.S. Army h played in the battle and placated everyo

Besides this, another move of Prime Minister's contributed to relievi the tension between S.H.A.E.F. and 21st Army Group. As operations in It had slowed down considerably, it w suggested that Alexander was bei wasted there. So Eisenhower's depu Tedder, was to be recalled to ordina R.A.F. service, his place being taken Alexander. Though this compromise not win Eisenhower's approval, it a came up against Montgomery's decid opposition. If he could not control ope tions himself, he did not want to see al body else get the job. From this point view, he thought that nothing should changed in the pattern of comma

Himmler's offensive

During the night of December 31/Janua

▷ *Armoured vehicles (in the foreground Stuart light tanks) of the French Foreign Legion parade through the streets of Strasbourg.*
△▷ *Strasbourg Cathedral on the day of the city's liberation.*

Himmler, as commander of Army Group *"Oberrhein"*, unleashed Operation *"Nordwind"*, giving his troops as objective the Saverne gap. In this way the American 7th Army would be cut in two and its fighting troops in the Bitche–Lauterbourg–Strasbourg salient annihilated. After the fast advance that Patton had been ordered to make on December 5, General Patch had had to extend his left flank as far as Saint Avold and, in the threatened sector, could only field VI Corps against eight German divisions, including the 21st Panzer and the 17th *"Götz von Berlichingen"* S.S. *Panzergrenadier* Divisions.

When he had redeployed as ordered (which stretched the seven divisions of the 7th Army over a front of 90 miles), the commander of the 6th Army Group, General Devers, had naturally been concerned about what to do in the event of a German offensive. In agreement with S.H.A.E.F., he had provided in such an event for his forces to fall back on the eastern slopes of the Vosges and the Belfort gap. This implied abandoning the plain of Alsace. In the afternoon of January 1, after a telephone call from Eisenhower, he issued the order to begin the movements planned for this eventuality.

de Gaulle disapproves

As Chief-of-Staff to the French Ministry of National Defence, General Juin had been advised since December 28 of the intentions of the 6th Army Group, confirmed by S.H.A.E.F. He had immediately informed General de Gaulle. The latter, seeing the possibility approach, wrote to General Eisenhower on January 1:

"For its part, the French Government cannot allow Strasbourg to fall into enemy hands again without doing everything in its power to defend it."

At the same time, he gave General de Lattre the following order:

"In the event of Allied forces falling

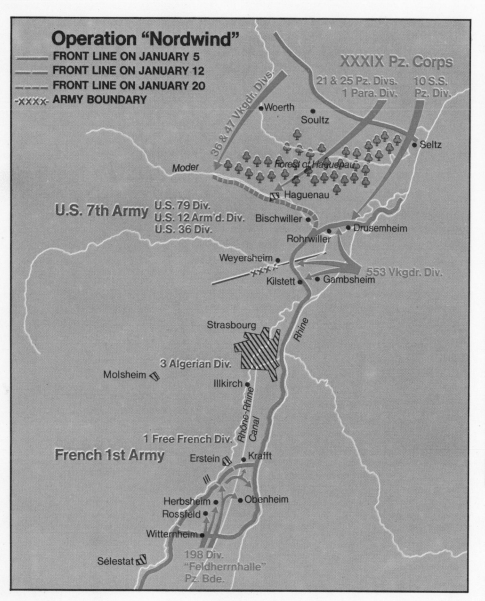

Operation "Nordwind"

— FRONT LINE ON JANUARY 5
-- FRONT LINE ON JANUARY 12
--- FRONT LINE ON JANUARY 20
-xxxx- ARMY BOUNDARY

XXXIX Pz. Corps

21 & 25 Pz. Divs.
1 Para. Div.

10 S.S.
Pz. Div.

36 & 47 Vkgdr. Divs.

• Woerth
Soultz

• Seltz

Moder

Forest of Haguenau

⬙ Haguenau

U.S. 7th Army

U.S. 79 Div.
U.S. 12 Arm'd. Div.
U.S. 36 Div.

Bischwiller •

• Drusemheim

Rohrwiller

Weyersheim •

553 Vkgdr. Div.

Kilstett • • Gambsheim

Rhine

Strasbourg

3 Algerian Div.

Molsheim ⬙

Illkirch •

French 1st Army

Rhône-Rhine Canal

1 Free French Div.

Erstein ⬙ • Krafft

III

Herbsheim • • Obenheim
Rossfeld •

Wittemheim •

Sélestat ⬙

198 Div.
"Feldherrnhalle"
Pz. Bde.

△ Operation "Nordwind", Reichsführer-S.S. Heinrich Himmler's ill-advised offensive against Strasbourg.
△▷ General de Lattre de Tassigny's proclamation to the citizens of Strasbourg on January 6, 1945. It called for calm and confidence, and pledged the French 1st Army to the successful defence of the city.

nevertheless seemed to want to he and assured me before I left that he wou try once more to convince his superic and I secured an interview for Gener. de Gaulle with General Eisenhower th next day."

On receiving the report prepared f him by Juin, de Gaulle once more appeale against the S.H.A.E.F. decision which he had just learned, affected not on] Strasbourg but the entire plain of Alsac In particular, he wrote to Eisenhower c January 3:

"In any case, I must confirm that th French Government cannot accept tha Alsace and a part of Lorraine should b intentionally evacuated without fighting so to speak, especially since the Frenc Army occupies most of the area. To agre to such an evacuation and in such cond tions would be an error from the point c view of the general conduct of the wa which stems not only from the militar command, but also from the Allied goverr ments. It would also be a serious errc from the French national point of view, t which the government is answerabl

"Therefore I have once more to instruc General de Lattre to use the French force he has to defend the positions he no

back from their present positions to the north of the French 1st Army, I instruct you to act on your own and take over the defence of Strasbourg."

These letters had gone when General de Gaulle was advised of the order to withdraw that had been circulated by General Devers. On receiving the news, he cabled President Roosevelt and the Prime Minister to make clear that he was opposed to evacuating Strasbourg and he instructed General Juin to express the same opinion at S.H.A.E.F.

The interview between Juin and General Bedell Smith, who met him the next day at S.H.A.E.F., was stormy, as was to be expected from two such plain-spoken men. There were even threats about what would happen if the French 1st Army removed itself from the authority of General Devers. All the same, noted Juin:

"Bedell Smith, who had blanched,

cupies and also to defend Strasbourg, even if the American forces on his left withdraw.

"From my point of view, I am extremely sorry that this disagreement has occurred a serious moment and I should like to hope that we can resolve our differences."

In *Crusade in Europe,* General Eisenhower mentions this incident and writes that:

"At first glance de Gaulle's argument seemed to be based upon political considerations founded more on emotion than on logic and consideration."

This represents the typical reasoning of the American strategist of the time, according to whom a military leader should not consider any objective but the destruction of the enemy's organised forces, without regard for political, geographical, sentimental, or prestige aims. In short, his thought regarding Strasbourg was the same as it had been before Paris the previous summer, and as it would be before Berlin three months later. Nevertheless, against this same point of view, he had to think of the consequences that a Franco-American crisis could have on Allied relations.

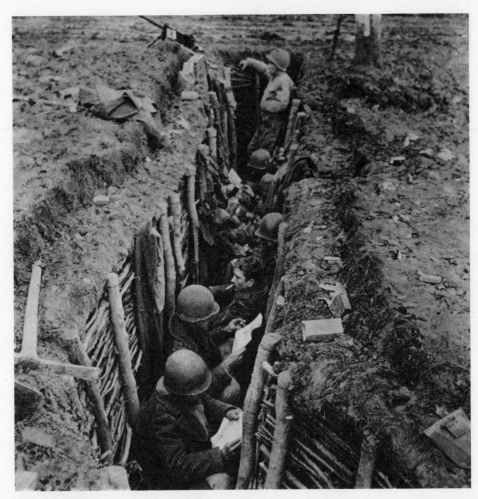

Churchill sides with de Gaulle

Churchill had been alerted by de Gaulle and, accompanied by Brooke, travelled to Paris. According to Brooke, they found Eisenhower "most depressed looking" when they walked down the steps from the plane, and it is certain that, at the lunch that followed, the Prime Minister was preaching to one already half-converted. A few hours later, Generals de Gaulle and Juin met Eisenhower, in the presence of Bedell Smith, Churchill, and Brooke, who noted that very evening:

"De Gaulle painted a gloomy picture of the massacres that would ensue if the Germans returned to portions of Alsace-Lorraine. However, Ike had already decided to alter his dispositions so as to leave the divisions practically where they were and not to withdraw the two divisions that were to have been moved up into Patton's reserve."

Juin confirms this: "When General de Gaulle and I arrived at Eisenhower's headquarters at Versailles . . . Churchill was already there. As soon as we came in

he informed us that it was all settled and that Strasbourg would not be abandoned. There was not even any discussion, and the only thing that was decided was that I should go with General Bedell Smith the next day to Vittel to inform General Devers, commanding the 6th Army Group."

Moreover, the tension between Eisenhower and de Gaulle eased so much as soon as this incident was settled that Eisenhower could not restrain himself from confiding to de Gaulle the difficulties he was having with Montgomery.

The battle for Strasbourg

Both on his own initiative and in virtue of the orders he received from Paris, General de Lattre was absolutely determined to hold Strasbourg. And so, on the night of January 2-3, he promptly sent in the solid 3rd Algerian Division, under the command of General du Vigier, recently appointed governor of the city. But, in spite of this, de Lattre intended to remain as long as he could under the control of General Devers and not make difficulties

△ *G.I.s catch up with their mail and with the news while waiting for the German offensive to break on them. Although he at first advocated the abandonment of the plain of Alsace, Eisenhower was at last persuaded by General de Gaulle's political objections to change his mind and order the American 7th Army to hold the Moder line.*

△ *"For whom tolls the bell?"*
"It tolls death for Hitler." And
with the Allies on the Rhine and
Oder, the defeat of the Third
Reich and Hitler's suicide were
only weeks away.

for inter-Allied strategy. That is why, at 2200 hours on January 3, he was very happy to receive the signal announcing that the 6th Army Group had received new orders.

As a result, the American VI Corps, between the Rhine and the Sarre, received orders to continue its retreat only as far as the Moder. But, on January 5, while VI Corps was digging in at this position and the 3rd Algerian Division completed its positions in Strasbourg, the 553rd *Volksgrenadier* Division crossed the Rhine at Gambsheim, between Strasbourg and the confluence of the Moder and Rhine. The next day, it was the turn of the German 19th Army to go over to the offensive, from the Colmar bridgehead. Pressing between the Ill and the Rhône-Rhine Canal, the *"Feldherrnhalle"* Panzer Brigade and the 198th Division managed to get as far as the Erstein heights, less than 13 miles from Strasbourg and 20 from the Gambsheim bridgehead that the 553rd Division had extended as far as the village of Killstett.

Around Strasbourg, attack and counter-attack followed ceaselessly. The Germans had forced the Moder a little above Haguenau and for a short time managed to establish a link with their 553rd Division. However, on January 26, they had definitely lost it again and the battlefield fell silent. O.B. West was very unhappy with the tactics Himmler had used in this offensive, for, instead of wearing down the enemy, he had wasted 11 divisions, four of them of the *Waffen*-S.S., frittering them away in piecemeal actions, ignoring the fact that the barrier of the Rhine prevented him from co-ordinating their movements. All the same, it was General Wiese who paid for the failure of *"Nordwind"*. He received the order to hand over command of the 19th Army to his comrade Rasp. As for Himmler, his flattering promotion to the command of Army Group "Vistula" led, on January 28, to the appointment of Colonel-General Hausser, still recuperating from the wounds he had received during the bloody fighting in the Falaise pocket, to command of Army Group *"Oberrhein"*.

In spite of Operation *"Nordwind"*, on January 15 de Lattre signed his "Personal and Secret Instruction Number 7":

"Leave the Germans no chance of escape. Free Colmar undamaged. The task consists of strangling the pocket alongside the Rhine where it receives its supplies, that is around Brisach.

"Two convergent wedges will be driv[en] in this direction. The first will go nort[h]-ward and will be made by Béthouart'[s] Corps, which will throw the enemy [off] balance and suck in his reserves. The[n] two days later, II Corps will go into actio[n]. This staggering is required by the time [it] will take to get the expected reserves in[to] place. Its effect will be to increase t[he] surprise of the enemy. Between the tw[o] offensive blocs, in the high Vosges, t[he] front will remain inactive at the begi[n]-ning. It will begin to move when our [line] along the Rhine is so tightly stretch[ed] that the fish is ready to be pulled in[.]

At this time, Devers and Eisenhow[er] were so concerned about cutting off t[he] Colmar pocket quickly that they did n[ot] hesitate to provide substantial reinforc[e]-ments for the French 1st Army: the U.[S.] 3rd Division remained under its comman[d] and it also received, though with certa[in] limitations, the 28th Division and t[he] 12th Armoured Division (Major-Genera[l] Norman D. Cota and Roderik R. Alle[n]) as well as the French 2nd Armour[ed] Division under Leclerc, transferred fro[m] the Strasbourg area specifically for t[his] purpose.

So, by January 20, 1945, the forc[es] available to de Lattre amounted to [?] divisions, four of which were armoure[d]. However, it should be pointed out that t[he] 3rd Algerian Division was still engag[ed] in and around Killstett and did not tak[e] part in the battle of Colmar and that, [in] the high Vosges, the newly-created 10t[h] Division (General Billotte) was restricte[d] to the modest rôle described abov[e.]

The German defence

Facing these forces along the 100-mil[e] long Alsace bridgehead, the German 19t[h] Army deployed its LXIV and LXIII Cor[ps] north and south under the comman[d] respectively, of General Thumm an[d] Lieutenant-General Abraham. The tw[o] corps had seven infantry or mountai[n] divisions and the 106th *"Feldherrnhalle"* Panzer Brigade. But these forces wer[e] threadbare. Including the reinforcement[s] attached to them, the best-equipped (th[e] 198th Division: Colonel Barde) ha[d] exactly 6,891 men in the line, and th[e] 716th *Volksgrenadier* Division (Colone[l] Hafner) had only 4,546. Furthermor[e,] although de Lattre complained abou[t] not receiving all the supplies he though[t]

The American Martin B-26G Marauder medium bomber

Engines : two Pratt & Whitney
R-2800-43 Twin Wasp radials,
1,920-hp each.
Armament : eleven .5-inch machine
guns and up to 4,000 lbs of bombs.
Speed : 283 mph at 5,000 feet.
Ceiling : 19,800 feet.
Range : 1,100 miles.
Weight empty/loaded :
25,300/38,200 lbs.
Span : 71 feet.
Length : 56 feet 1 inch.
Height : 20 feet 4 inches.
Crew : 7.

An M3 half-track of the French 1st Army moves into Colmar on February 2, 1945. ▷▷ A mine explodes in the path of an M10 tank destroyer of a French armoured division, fully equipped with the latest U.S. matériel.

"Our armies are marching with all despatch to the East and to the West . . ." "Is that really true?" "Yes, mein Führer, the ones on the Western Front to the East, and the ones on the Eastern Front to the West!"

he needed, by the eighth day of battle General Rasp was reduced to ordering strict economy to his gunners: 12 15-cm and 15 10.5-cm shells per day per gun, compared with 90 155-mm and 120 105-mm shells in the French 1st Army.

Three circumstances, however, compensated a little for the numerical and *matériel* inferiority of the defenders:

1. the terrain, which was no more than "a network of streams and rivers" according to de Lattre. Within it are many woods and even more villages, among which should be mentioned the manufacturing and industrial towns of the Mulhouse region;

2. the weather. On the first day, I Corps attacked LXIII Corps in the face of a snowstorm blowing from the northeast. At night, the temperature fell to 20 and even 25 degrees Centigrade below zero. Finally, just when German resistance was softening, an unexpected rise in the temperature swelled the rivers and made the roads into sloughs of mud; and

3. though far less numerous, the Panther tanks and *"Jagdpanther"* and *"Nashorn"* tank destroyers, with their very high velocity 8.8-cm guns, were far superior to the French 1st Army's Sherman tanks and M10 tank destroyers. This superiority was emphasised by the German vehicles' wide tracks, which allowed them to manoeuvre on the snow in weather conditions with which their opponents

were not able to cope.

At 0700 hours on January 20, H-ho sounded for the reinforced I Corps. task was to break the enemy line betwee Thann and the Forest of Nünenbruc to capture Cernay, and then to push without stopping towards Ensisheim ai Réguisheim on the Ill. For this purpos over a 14-mile front, Béthouart had t 9th Colonial Division (General Morlièr around Mulhouse, the 2nd Moroccc Division (General Carpentier) in t centre, and the 4th Moroccan Mounta Division (General de Hesdin) arou Thann. In spite of the support of the tan of the 1st Armoured Division (Gener Sudre), the attempt to break the enen lines towards Cernay was not very succe ful, both because of the tough resistan met, aided by well-sited minefields, a because of the snowstorms which ma artillery observation impossible.

On the other hand, the seconda attack, which had been entrusted to t 9th Colonial Division, took the villages Burtzwiller, Illzach, Kingersheir Pfastadt, and Lutterbach, a remarkab success due to the dash with whic General Salan had led the infantry of th division.

On the following day, LXIII Cor counter-attacked and, on January 2 with the storm blowing worse than eve General Béthouart expressed the opinic that they should wait for it to blow itse out. But any let-up on the part of I Cor would have prejudiced the attack of

orps, which was just finishing its pre-
arations. So Béthouart was ordered to
ress on with his attack, and a fierce,
tter struggle was waged close to Wittel-
eim, in the Forest of Nünenbruck, and
r the factory towns with their potassium
eposits. These towns had to be cleared
e by one.

he Colmar pocket
iped out

n January 23, II Corps, still under the
mmand of General G. de Monsabert,
rced a second wedge into the German
ne. This was achieved with more ease
an the first, even though General
asp had got wind of the French plans.
On the right, the American 3rd Division
ad taken Ostheim. On the left, the 1st
ree French Division had fought bitterly
capture the village of Illhausern and
ad formed a bridgehead on the right
ank of the Ill, thus preparing to out-
ank Colmar to the north. But LXIV
orps stiffened its resistance and counter-
tacked, preventing Monsabert from
ny swift exploitation of his success to-
ards Neuf-Brisach. LXIII Corps was
kewise preventing Béthouart from mov-
g on. Hidden in the woods, or even inside
ouses, the Panzers exacted a heavy toll
om the men of the 2nd and 5th Armoured
ivisions, supporting the infantry. How-
er, on January 27, the U.S. 3rd Division
ached the Colmar Canal, while General
arbay's 1st Free French Division, re-
forced by Colonel Faure's paratroops,
ok the villages of Jebsheim and Grussen-
eim. Seeing how serious the situation
ad become, O.K.W. authorised Rasp
pull the 198th Division back over the
hine, i.e. to give up all the ground won
etween Rhinau and Erstein by the
ttack of January 7.
Wishing to press on and complete the
ttack, General Devers, at the request
f the commander of the French 1st
rmy, put XXI Corps (Major-General
rank W. Milburn) under his command,
well as the U.S. 75th Division (Major-
eneral Porter). Milburn, who from this
me on commanded all the American
rces involved in the offensive, and the
rench 5th Armoured Division, was
rdered to position his forces between
onsabert's II Corps and Billotte's 10th
ivision, and then push on towards Neuf-

△ *General Emile Béthouart, commander of the French I Corps. Operating on the south side of the Colmar pocket, his troops initially had a very hard time of it, and Béthouart wished to call off his attack. But de Lattre ordered him to press on regardless so that German forces would not be able to switch to the northern sector, where General de Monsabert's II Corps was about to launch its offensive.*

Brisach and also south towards Ensisheim to meet Béthouart. The offensive began again. In the evening of January 30, after a terrifying artillery bombardment of 16,438 105-mm and 155-mm shells, the United States 3rd Division (Major-General O'Daniel) succeeded in crossing the Colmar Canal, and this allowed the United States 28th Division to advance as far as the suburbs of Colmar. The division did not enter Colmar itself, for at the gates of the city, which had been left intact, General Norman D. Cota was courteous enough to give that honour to his comrade-in-arms Schlesser, commanding the 4th Combat Command (5th Armoured Division).

The United States 12th Armoured Division sped south to exploit its victory, with the intention of linking up with I Corps, which had taken Ensisheim, Soultz, and Guebwiller on February 4 and then pushed its 1st Armoured Division and 4th Moroccan Mountain Division forward.

The next day, French and American forces linked up at Rouffach and Sainte Croix-en-Plaine. Twenty-four hours later, in the light of searchlights shining towards the night sky, General O'Daniel's infantry "scaled" the ramparts of Neuf-Brisach in the best mediaeval style. Lastly, at 0800 hours on February 9, a deafening explosion told the men of the French 1st and 2nd Armoured Divisions, who were mopping-up the Forest of la Hardt, together with the 2nd Moroccan Division, that the Germans had just blown the Chalampé bridge, on the Mulhouse–Freiburg road, behind them as they pulled back over the Rhine.

And so, at dawn on the 20th day, the battle of Colmar reached its end. General Rasp left 22,010 prisoners, 80 guns, and 70 tanks in the hands of the enemy, but he had succeeded in bringing back over the Rhine some 50,000 men, 7,000 motor vehicles, 1,500 guns, and 60 armoured vehicles, which underlines his personal qualities of leadership.

As for Allied losses, the figures provided by General de Lattre will allow the reader to appreciate the cost of a modern battle. Of a total of 420,000 Allied troops involved (295,000 French, 125,000 American), casualties were as follows:

	French	American
Killed	1,595	542
Wounded	8,583	2,670
Sick	3,887	3,228
Totals	14,065	6,440

Considering just the French, de Lattre figures also show that the infantry ha taken the lion's share. On January 2 it had put 60,000 men into the line, that about a fifth of the men in the 1st Arm On February 9, it could own to thre quarters of the losses, with 1,138 kille and 6,513 wounded. Add to these figur the 354 killed and 1,151 wounded whic the battle cost the armoured units, a it becomes clear that the other arms lo only 1,022 killed and wounded. Finall due credit must be given to the magnifice effort of the medical services und Surgeon-General Guirriec. In spite the appalling weather they had on 142 deaths, that is 0.9 per cent of the cas received.

As a conclusion to the story of th battle, some tribute should be paid to th men who fought in it. In the *Revue militai suisse*, Major-General Montfort ha written:

"The French, under superb leadersh and enjoying powerful *matériel* adva tages, made a magnificent effort, ful worthy of their predecessors in Wor War I.

"The Germans, under extraordinari difficult conditions and three differin requirements (operational, *matériel*, an morale), defended themselves with grea ability and fought . . . with courage worth of praise."

Montgomery and Eisenhower clash again

It should be noted that there had bee much inter-Allied squabbling about th length of time that the battle for Colma was taking: the Allied high comman wanted this irritating pocket cleared ou of the way as quickly as possible, so tha all available Allied forces might b readied for the last devastating blo against Germany that would win the wa in the West. The irritation caused by th Colmar delay was perhaps exacerbate by another clash between Eisenhowe and Montgomery. But what increase the trouble even more was the fact tha Brooke backed Montgomery with all th weight of his authority. Once mor S.H.A.E.F. and the 21st Army Grou were divided on the alternatives of th "concentrated push" or the "wide front"

Eisenhower rejected Montgomery's in

△ Shermans of the French 1st Army push on towards the Rhine after the liberation of Colmar.

tion of supervising Bradley's operations, but nevertheless, on December 31, 44, informed Montgomery of his plan of erations:

"Basic plan–to destroy enemy forces st of Rhine, north of the Moselle, and prepare for crossing the Rhine in rce with the *main effort north of the hr.*"

Once the Ardennes salient had been iched out (Point *a*), Eisenhower enaged the following general offensive:

"*b*. Thereafter First and Third Armies drive to north-east on general line um-Bonn, eventually to Rhine.

"*c*. When *a* is accomplished, 21st Army oup, with Ninth U.S. Army under erational command, to resume pre- rations for 'Veritable'."

In practical terms, this plan required ontgomery to force the Reichswald rest position, which bars the corridor tween the Maas and the Rhine on the ttch-German frontier, to secure the t bank of the Rhine between Emmerich d Düsseldorf, and to prepare to force a ssage of the river north of its junction th the Ruhr. This sketch of a plan eased Montgomery, who wrote:

"It did all I wanted except in the realm operational control, and because of arshall's telegram that subject was

closed. It put the weight in the north and gave the Ninth American Army to 21 Army Group. It gave me power of decision in the event of disagreement with Bradley on the boundary between 12 and 21 Army Groups. In fact, I had been given very nearly all that I had been asking for since August. Better late than never. I obviously could not ask for more."

Nevertheless, when one considers the allotment of forces and in particular the fixing of objectives, there is no avoiding the fact that the two sides did not speak a common language any more.

Actually, Montgomery estimated that if "Veritable" was to be successful, American reinforcements should consist of five corps, (16 divisions), of which four corps (13 divisions) should be placed under the command of the American 9th Army, and the rest under the British 2nd Army. In these estimates, he seems to have been completely unaware of the principles established by his superior at the beginning of his outline dated December 31: "to destroy enemy forces west of Rhine". According to Eisenhower's clearly-expressed opinion, this required a second push from around Prüm towards the Rhine at Bonn, which would reduce the United States forces which could be detached for "Veritable"

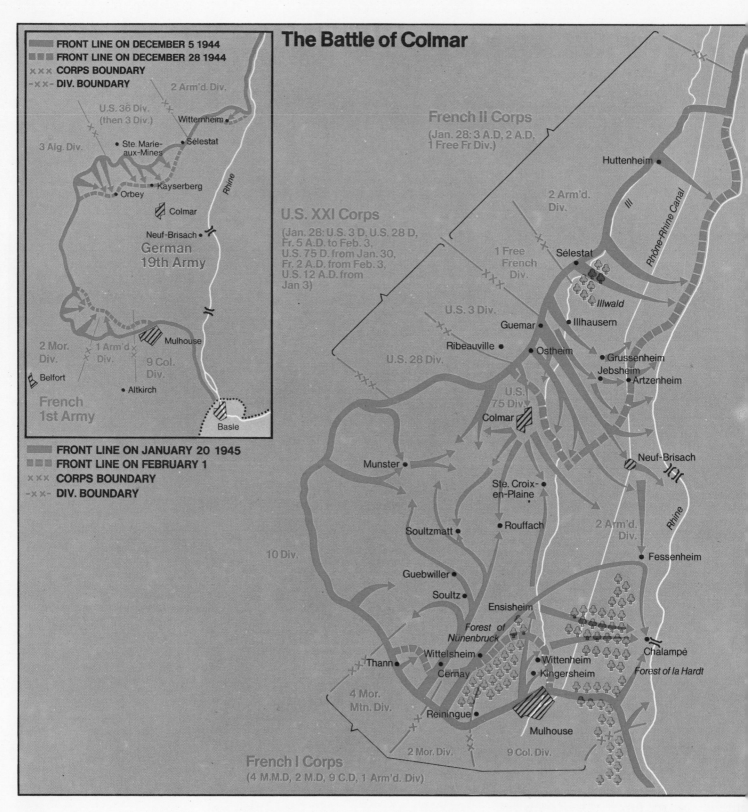

The Battle of Colmar

Legend (top box):
- FRONT LINE ON DECEMBER 5 1944
- FRONT LINE ON DECEMBER 28 1944
- ××× CORPS BOUNDARY
- -××- DIV. BOUNDARY

**Inset map labels:**
2 Arm'd. Div.
U.S. 36 Div. (then 3 Div.)
3 Alg. Div.
Witternheim
Ste. Marie-aux-Mines
Sélestat
Kayserberg
Orbey
Colmar
Rhine
Neuf-Brisach
German 19th Army
2 Mor. Div.
1 Arm'd Div.
9 Col. Div.
Mulhouse
Belfort
Altkirch
French 1st Army
Basle

Legend (lower box):
- FRONT LINE ON JANUARY 20 1945
- FRONT LINE ON FEBRUARY 1
- ××× CORPS BOUNDARY
- -××- DIV. BOUNDARY

**Main map labels:**
French II Corps (Jan. 28: 3 A.D, 2 A.D, 1 Free Fr Div.)
Huttenheim
2 Arm'd. Div.
Ill
Rhône-Rhine Canal
U.S. XXI Corps (Jan. 28: U.S. 3 D, U.S. 28 D, Fr. 5 A.D. to Feb. 3, U.S. 75 D. from Jan. 30, Fr. 2 A.D. from Feb. 3, U.S. 12 A.D. from Jan 3)
Sélestat
1 Free French Div.
Illwald
U.S. 3 Div.
Guemar
Illhausern
Ribeauville
Ostheim
Grussenheim
Jebsheim
Artzenheim
U.S. 28 Div.
U.S. 75 Div.
Colmar
Munster
Neuf-Brisach
Ste. Croix-en-Plaine
Rhine
2 Arm'd. Div.
Soultzmatt
Rouffach
Fessenheim
10 Div.
Guebwiller
Soultz
Ensisheim
Chalampé
Forest of Nunenbruck
Forest of la Hardt
Wittelsheim
Wittenheim
Thann
Cernay
Kingersheim
4 Mor. Mtn. Div.
Reiningue
Mulhouse
2 Mor. Div.
9 Col. Div.
French I Corps (4 M.M.D, 2 M.D, 9 C.D, 1 Arm'd. Div)

△ *The French 1st Army's battle to eliminate the German 19th Army's pocket around Colmar.*

to only three corps and 12 divisions. Montgomery was obliged to give in, but he resumed the argument on January 20 when he heard the news that Bradley, far from limiting himself to reducing the Ardennes salient, intended to follow up his attack for another fortnight. Montgomery wrote to Brooke:

"Both Ike and Bradley are emphatic that we should not–not–cross the Rhine in strength anywhere until we are lined up along its entire length from Nijmeg to Switzerland."

Two days later, in a second letter whi like the first, he has not quoted in memoirs, he harped on the same questio

"My latest information is th S.H.A.E.F. are very worried about sit tion in South about Colmar and Str bourg..."

As the commander-in-chief seem ready to reinforce this sector, it follow

at "Veritable" would be postponed
definitely. This led him to conclude
bitterly:

"I fear that the old snags of indecision
and vacillation and refusal to consider
the military problem fairly and squarely
are coming to the front again . . . The real
trouble is that there is no control and the
three Army Groups are each intent on
their own affairs. Patton to-day issued a
stirring order to Third Army, saying the
next step would be Cologne . . . one has to
preserve a sense of humour these days,
otherwise one would go mad."

Support for Eisenhower

Brooke was appreciative of this argument
and "cordially, but very gravely", as
General Eisenhower writes, expressed
the view to him that putting his plan into
effect would have the result of producing
an "organised dispersion" of Allied forces.
Eisenhower opposed this view, and events
proved him right. First of all, the Germans had to be deprived of the advantage
of permanent fortifications which allowed
them to economise their means and then
build up massive forces in the sector
where the main attack would be launched:
"If, however, we should first, in a series
of concentrated and powerful attacks,
destroy the German forces west of the
Rhine, the effect would be to give us all
along the great front a defensive line of
equal strength to the enemy's. We calculated that with the western bank of
the Rhine in our possession we could hurl
some seventy-five reinforced divisions
against the German in great converging
attacks. If we allowed the enemy south of
the Ruhr to remain in the Siegfried, we
would be limited to a single offensive by
some thirty-five divisions.

"A second advantage of our plan would
be the deflection of the enemy forces later
to be met at the crossings of the Rhine
obstacle. Moreover, the effect of the
converging attack is multiplied when it
is accompanied by such air power as we
had in Europe in the early months of
1945. Through its use we could prevent
the enemy from switching forces back
and forth at will against either of the
attacking columns and we could likewise employ our entire air power at any
moment to further the advance in any
area desired."

But although Eisenhower had refuted

Brooke's point, he was unable to convert
the latter to his way of thinking. That is
why he travelled to Marseilles on January
25 to explain to Marshall, who was on his
way to Yalta via Malta, his plan of operations and the objections it was coming
up against among the British. He had no
difficulty in obtaining Marshall's complete agreement, and the latter said to
him at the end of the interview:

"I can, of course, uphold your position
merely on the principle that these decisions fall within your sphere of responsibility. But your plan is so sound that I
think it better for you to send General
Smith to Malta so that he may explain
these matters in detail. Their logic will
be convincing."

This was done and, after some explana-
tions by Bedell Smith and some amend-
ments on the part of the Combined Chiefs-
of-Staff Committee, Eisenhower's plan,
comprising of a double push towards the
Rhine and a double encirclement of the
Ruhr, was adopted and Montgomery
would spare nothing to make it a success.

△ △ *American infantry move up
through a snowstorm, typical of
the weather that helped the
Germans considerably at the
beginning of 1945.*
△ *General Marshall, head of the
U.S. Army, arrives in Malta
en route to Yalta. Marshall
sided firmly with Eisenhower in
the dispute the latter was having
with Montgomery.*

△ *Evidence of American artillery superiority: a destroyed German triple 2-cm self-propelled mounting.*

CHAPTER 146
Remagen Bridge

On January 16, the American 3rd and 1st Armies crushed the tip of the Ardennes salient and linked up in the ruins of Houffalize. The following day, as agreed, the 1st Army was returned to the command of Bradley, to his great satisfaction. But he was far less pleased with the task now given him, that of engaging the Germans in the wooded and hilly region of Schleiden and Schmidt, which had cost him so dear the previous autumn, and of capturing the hydro-electric system of the Rur, the Erft, and the Olef. On February 8, V Corps (under Major-General

L. T. Gerow), of the 1st Army had reach its objective. That was that. At dawn, the next day, the Germans blew up t reservoir gates and from mid-day onwar the water was rising at a rate of near two and a half feet an hour in front of t 9th Army.

Meanwhile, the left of this army, st under the command of Lieutenan General William H. Simpson, and t right of the British 2nd Army, und General Miles C. Dempsey, were taki out the salient which the enemy w holding between the Maas and the Ru w an enclave between the Allied flanks. e little Dutch village of Roermond was ll held by the German 15th Army, ich formed the right of Army Group ". On January 28, this rectifying eration, a prelude to the pincer attack lled "Veritable/Grenade", was brought a successful conclusion.

undstedt powerless

this duel between Field-Marshal von ndstedt and General Eisenhower, the mer had at his disposal at the beginning February (after he had lost the 6th nzerarmee, taken away to help the ngarian front), 73 divisions, including ht Panzer or *Panzergrenadier*. But e infantry divisions had fallen to an

average of about 7,000 men each. As for the armoured formations, whatever may have been the excellent quality of their *matériel*, they suffered a continual shortage of petrol. In other words, as had started to become evident in the battle of Colmar, the crisis in munitions was getting ever more desperate at the front. The land forces of the Third Reich, moreover, could not rely on any support from the Luftwaffe, whose jet fighters were fully engaged attempting to defend what

△ *Montgomery* (standing, right) *confers with Horrocks* (standing, left). *Note the insignia on the jeep: four stars, signifying that the owner was a general, and the badge of the 21st Army Group. This latter was a blue cross on a red shield, with two crossed golden swords superimposed.*

△ As the Allies pushed on to
the Rhine, the cities of Germany
continued to suffer under the
day and night efforts of the
U.S. 8th and 15th Air Forces
and R.A.F. Bomber Command.
These are the gutted remains of
Stuttgart.

was left of Germany's cities against the redoubled attacks of the British and American Strategic Air Forces.

The last straw was that Rundstedt, in his office at Koblenz, was faced by a hopeless situation, and had been stripped of all initiative in the direction of operations. On January 21, he received the following incredible *Führerbefehl*, with orders to distribute it down to divisional level:

"Commanders-in-chief, army, corps, and divisional commanders are personally responsible to me for reporting in good time:

"(a) Every decision to execute an operational movement.

"(b) Every offensive plan from divisional level upwards that does not fit exactly with the directives of the higher command.

"(c) Every attack in a quiet sector intended to draw the enemy's attention to that sector, with the exception of normal shock troop actions.

"(d) Every plan for withdrawal or retreat.

"(e) Every intention of surrendering a position, a strongpoint, or a fortress.

"Commanders must make sure that I have time to intervene as I see fit, and that my orders can reach the front line troops in good time."

And the *Führer* further announc
that any commander or staff officer wh
by "deliberate intent, carelessness,
oversight" hindered the execution
this order, would be punished with "dr
conian severity".

Allied superiority

From the Swiss frontier to the Nor
Sea, Eisenhower had 70 divisions und
his command on January 1, 1945:

	Infantry	Armoured	Airborne	Total
U.S.	31	11	3	45
British	7	4	1	12
Canadian	2	1	–	3
French	6	3	–	9
Polish	–	1	–	1
Totals	46	20	4	70

By May 8 this number would have be
increased by another 15 American div
sions (including four armoured), s
French divisions, and two Canadi
divisions (including one armoured).

Deducting six divisions fighting in t
Alps or besieging German fortresse
this would give S.H.A.E.F. 87 divisio
at the end of the war.

Despite the losses they had to bear, t

Allied divisions at this time were far less restricted than their German counterparts. The supply crisis, so acute in September, was now no more than an unpleasant memory. Petrol was in good supply and there was no shortage of shells at the front. The proximity fuses with which they were fitted allowed the gunners to fire shells which burst in the air, wreaking havoc among exposed troops. With reference to armour, the introduction into the United States Army of the heavy (41-ton) M26 General Pershing tank was significant. It was well-armoured, and had a 90-mm gun and good cross-country performance, the result of its Christie-type suspension and wide tracks. The Americans had rediscovered this suspension after seeing the results it gave in the service of the Germans, who had borrowed the idea from the Russians. The latter had acquired a licence to build the Christie suspension from the United States, after 1919, when the American military authorities had refused, in spite of the urging of the young Major George S. Patton, to take any firm interest in Christie and his advanced designs.

Thus the Allies' land forces were far more numerous than the Germans'. They also enjoyed powerful air support from a force which was both numerous and well-trained. Here General Devers had the Franco-American 1st Tactical Air Force (Major-General R. M. Webster), in which the French I Air Corps (Brigadier-General Gerardot) was itself attached to the French 1st Army. The United States 9th Air Force (Lieutenant-General Hoyt S. Vandenberg,) came under the overall command of General Bradley, and the British 2nd Tactical Air Force (Air-Marshal Sir Arthur Coningham) efficiently seconded Field-Marshal Montgomery's operations. On the German side there was nothing which could resist this formidable mass of flying artillery.

On November 12, 1944, 28 R.A.F. Lancasters attacked the great battleship *Tirpitz* in Tromsö with 12,000-lb "Tallboy" bombs and sank her at her anchorage. What was now left of the surface forces of the Kriegsmarine was being expended in the Baltic in attempts to help the army. As for the U-boats, which had lost 242 of their number during 1944, their successes in the North Atlantic between June 6, 1944 and May 8, 1945, were limited to the sinking of 31 merchant ships, displacing

altogether only 178,000 tons. This was virtually nothing at all.

Complete surprise

At 0500 hours on February 8, 1,400 guns of the Canadian 1st Army blasted the German 84th Division, which had dug itself in along a seven-mile front between the Maas and the Waal close to the Dutch-German frontier. At 1030 hours, the British XXX Corps, which Montgomery had put under the command of General Crerar, moved in to the attack with five divisions (the British 51st, 53rd, and 15th and the Canadian 2nd and 3rd) in the first wave and the 43rd Division and the Guards Armoured Division in reserve. In all, according to the commander of the corps, Lieutenant-General Horrocks, there were 200,000 men and 35,000 vehicles.

The German position was heavily mined, and included a flooded area on the right and the thick Reichswald forest on the left. Moreover, the day before the attack, a thaw had softened the ground. Neither Hitler, at O.K.W., nor Colonel-General Blaskowitz, commanding Army Group "H", had been willing to accept the idea that Montgomery would choose such a sector in which to attack. Yet

General Schlemm, commanding the 1st Parachute Army, had warned them of this possibility. At the end of the day the 84th Division had lost 1,300 prisoners and was close to breaking-point.

Meanwhile the American 9th Army had been ordered to unleash Operation "Grenade" on February 10. This would cross the Rur and advance to the Rhine at Düsseldorf. Now came the flooding caused by the destruction of the Eifel dams, which held up the American 9th Army completely for 12 days and slowed down the British XXX Corps. The latter's units were also hopelessly mixed up. These delays allowed Schlemm to send his 7th and 6th Parachute, 15th *Panzer-grenadier,* and then 116th Panzer Divisions to the rescue one after the other. And as Colonel C. P. Stacey, the official Canadian Army historian, notes, the Germans, at the edge of the abyss, had lost none of their morale:

"In this, the twilight of their gods, the defenders of the Reich displayed the recklessness of fanaticism and the courage of despair. In the contests west of the Rhine, in particular, they fought with special ferocity and resolution, rendering the battles in the Reichswald and Hochwald forests grimly memorable in the annals of this war."

On February 13, the Canadian 1st Army had mopped up the Reichswald and the little town of Kleve, and had reached Gennep, where it was reinforced across the Maas by the British 52nd Division and 11th Armoured Division. Schlemm threw two divisions of infantry into the battle as well as the famous Panzer *"Lehr"* Division, and so the intervention of Lieutenant-General G. G. Simonds' Canadian II Corps at the side of the British XXX Corps did not have the decisive effect that Crerar expected. The 11th day of the offensive saw the attackers marking time on the Goch–Kalkar line about 1 miles from their jumping-off point.

▽ *The end of the* Tirpitz, *Germany's second and last battleship. Lying capsized in Tromsö fjord, with small vessels moored by her keel, she looks more like an island than a once-proud capital ship.*

But, just like the British 2nd Army in Normandy, the Canadian 1st Army had attracted the larger part of the enemy's forces, while the flood water in the Rur valley was going down. The weather also turned finer, and Montgomery fixed February 23 for the launching of Operation "Grenade". In his order of the day to the men of the 21st Army Group, Montgomery assured them that this was to be the beginning of the last round against Germany. The Third Reich was ready for the knock-out blow, which would be delivered from several directions.

Then, as an opening move, the Anglo-American Strategic Air Force launched 9000 bombers and fighter-bombers and made the heaviest attack of the war on the Third Reich's communications network.

More than 200 targets featured on the programme of this attack, which went under the name of Operation "Clarion". Some of these objectives were bombed from only 4,500 feet because enemy anti-aircraft action was almost totally in-effective since Hitler had stripped it to supply the Eastern Front. The results of this bombing on February 22 were still noticeable when Colonel-General Jodl came to bring General Eisenhower the surrender of the Third Reich.

The following day, at 0245 hours, the artillery of the United States 9th Army opened fire on German positions on the Rur. The 15th Army (General von Zangen) which defended them, formed the right of Army Group "B" (Field-Marshal Model). Though it defended itself well, his 353rd Division was still thrown out of the ruins of Julich by the American XIX Corps (Major-General Raymond S. Maclain). Meanwhile, in the Linnich sector, XIII Corps (Major-General Alvan C. Gillem) had established a bridgehead a mile and a half deep. VII Corps (Lieutenant-General John L. Collins) of the American 1st Army, had also taken part in the attack and, by the end of the day, had mopped up Duren.

Hitler, Rundstedt, and Model used every last resource to tackle this new crisis looming on the horizon. Schlemm was stripped of the reinforcements which had just been despatched to him, and to these were added the 9th and 11th Panzer Divisions and the 3rd *Panzergrenadier* Division. These forces were instructed to hit the enemy's north-easterly push in its flank.

All the same, by February 27, the Allied breakthrough was complete near Erkelenz, and two days later, XIII Corps swept through the conurbation of Rheydt –Mönchengladbach. At the same time, to the right of the 9th Army, XVI Corps (Major-General J. B. Anderson) hurtled towards Roermond and Venlo behind the 1st Parachute Army, while on the right, XIX Corps was approaching Neuss opposite Düsseldorf.

In these circumstances Schlemm was ordered to retreat to the right bank of the Rhine, and he must be given all credit for carrying out this delicate and dangerous mission with remarkable skill. Rearguard skirmishes at Rheinberg, Sonsbeck, and Xanten gave him the time to get the bulk of his forces across and to complete the planned demolitions without fault. On March 6, the United States 9th Army and the Canadian 1st Army linked up opposite Wesel.

This joint Operation "Veritable/Grenade" cost the 18 German divisions

△ *The "Masters of the World" return home.*

The British Hawker Tempest V Series 1 fighter and fighter-bomber

Engine: one Napier Sabre IIB inline, 2,200-hp.
Armament: four 20-mm Hispano Mark II cannon with 200 rounds per gun, plus two 1,000-lb bombs or eight 60-lb rockets.
Speed: 435 mph at 17,000 feet.
Climb: 6 minutes 6 seconds to 20,000 feet.
Ceiling: 36,000 feet.
Range: 1,300 miles with drop tanks.
Weight empty/loaded: 9,250/11,400 lbs.
Span: 41 feet.
Length: 33 feet 8 inches.
Height: 16 feet 1 inch.

gaged 53,000 prisoners. But Crerar one had suffered 15,634 dead, wounded, d missing, of which 5,304 were Canadian oops.

On that same day, March 6, the leading vision of the American VII Corps tered Cologne. Now the Allies were ing the Rhine between Cologne and ijmegen, more than 100 miles down-ream, where the river, if the stream ows down, widens to reach a breadth great as 250 or 300 yards, and all the idges had been destroyed. Forcing e Rhine north of the Ruhr, according Montgomery's formula, would result a delay of two weeks and necessitate nsiderable reinforcements for the 21st rmy Group. And here can be seen Eisen-ower's farsightedness in keeping to s plan of operations of December 31, 44: to defeat the enemy west of the ine. For, if he had kept Bradley marking ne then, Hitler could have detached the rces necessary to check Montgomery the Rhine below Cologne.

This did not happen, for, on March 6, rmy Group "B" was fighting the Ameri-n 1st Army on its right and the 3rd on centre. Its 5th *Panzerarmee* (Colonel-eneral Harpe) was now well and truly tflanked and overrun on both wings. ccording to the original plan, the Ameri-n 1st Army was to provide the left flank Operation "Grenade". With this in ew, General Bradley had increased its e to three corps (14 divisions). But it as not foreseen that the 3rd Army would ke part in the attack and it was only by rather surreptitious move that, during e second week of January, Patton had ished his forces as far as the Moselle Luxembourg, the Sûre, and the Our ar the *Westwall,* covering himself at H.A.E.F. by claiming that his moves ere "offensive defence", when his gression had no other aim but that of aching the Rhine at Koblenz.

The defeat of the German 15th Army ened a breach in Field-Marshal Model's e which General Hodges and his 1st rmy did not delay in exploiting. Having cupied Cologne, VII Corps set off for nn on March 7. III Corps (Major-eneral J. Millikin), which was advanc-g on the right of VII Corps, had orders take the crossings over the Ahr. This sk was entrusted to the 9th Armoured ivision (Major-General John W. onard).

Towards the end of the morning of arch 7, Brigadier-General William M.

Hoge, leading Combat Command "B" of the 9th Armoured Division, was informed that the Ludendorff Bridge near Remagen was still intact. He decided not to follow his orders (which had specified Sinzig as his target) to the letter and resolved there and then to chance his luck and seize the bridge. A little before 1600 hours, 2nd Lieutenant Karl Timmermann ventured on to the bridge, followed by the Burrows section. Seeing them, the German guard tried to set off the demoli-tion charges, but in vain. Under American fire, Sergeant Faust, another hero of this episode, then lit the fuse. But the effect of the explosion was insignificant, and, a few minutes later, Sergeant Alex Drabik was the first American fighting man to step on the right bank of the Rhine. Be-hind him, Lieutenant Hugh B. Mott, a combat engineer, and three sappers tore the charges from the girders and threw the explosives into the river.

"The enemy had reached Kreuzberg and as far as a bridge near Remagen which, it appears, was encumbered with fugitives. They crossed the bridge and succeeded in forming a bridgehead on the eastern bank of the river. Counter-attack early this morning. The 11th Panzer Division will be brought from Bonn. But petrol is in short supply."

The O.K.W. war diary records this national catastrophe in these unemotional words. Therefore it gives no account of Hitler's rage, which was terrible. Major Scheler and three others were declared responsible, on Hitler's orders, for the success of the Allied surprise attack, court-martialled, and shot.

Twenty-four hours after this surprise, there were already 8,000 Americans in the bridgehead. By March 17, four divi-sions (9th, 78th, 99th, and 9th Armoured) were dug in. On the same day the bridge collapsed. Hitler had concentrated the fire of a battery of 17-cm guns on it, as well as ordering aircraft and V-2 attacks, and even attempts by Kriegsmarine human torpedoes and frogmen. But, protected by booms and nets, 1st Army engineers had already built another bridge and both banks of the Rhine were bristling with anti-aircraft guns.

Having transferred III Corps (three divi-sions) to the 1st Army, Patton remained in command of VIII, XII, and XX Corps, which had 12 divisions, three of which were armoured. The crossing of the Our and the Sûre, on the Saint Vith–Echter-nach line, was no little matter because

△ *The nemesis of Germany's civilian bombing campaigns early in the war: the avenging angel of the British and American strategic bombing forces.*

the rivers were in flood. The forcing of *Westwall* was also very tough. In XII Corps there was one division which had to reduce 120 concrete casemates. This it did with self-propelled 155-mm guns, pounding the embrasures from a range of only 300 yards.

In spite of everything, by the end of February VIII and XII Corps were on the Kyll, having advanced about 20 miles into German territory. XX Corps had taken Saarburg and advanced as far as the apex of the triangle formed by the Mosel and the Saar at their confluence a little above Trier. Up till then the German 7th Army (General Brandenberger), which faced Patton, had defended itself tenaciously, but this very tenacity explains why, on March 1, having exhausted its supplies, it literally collapsed. On that day, wrote Patton:

"At 14.15, Walker [commander of XX Corps] called up to say the 10th Armoured Division was in Trier and had captured a bridge over the Moselle intact. The capture of this bridge was due to the heroic act of Lieutenant Colonel J. J. Richardson, deceased. He was riding in the leading vehicle of his battalion of armoured infantry when he saw the wires leading to the demolition charges at the far end of the bridge. Jumping out of the vehicle, he raced across the bridge under heavy fire and cut the wires. The acid test of battle brings out the pure metal."

On March 3, the forcing of the Kyll at Kyllburg by the 5th Division, under Major-General S. LeRoy Irwin, enabled Major-General Manton Eddy, commanding XII Corps, to detach his 4th Division. Under the command of Major-General Hugh J. Gaffey, this division made a raid of mad audacity, covering 26 miles on March 4 alone and reaching Daun in the evening. Two days later, it reached the Rhine above Koblenz. On its left, the 11th Armoured Division (Major-General Holmes E. Dager), advancing ahead of VII Corps, established first contact with the American 1st Army on March 11, near Brohl.

On March 8, the O.K.W. war diary noted that LIII Corps had been steamrollered and that any co-ordinated conduct of operations was henceforth impossible. The truth of this is illustrated by the capture of General von Rothkirch und Panthen, in command of LIII Corps. Bradley recounts the story thus:

"So rapid was the dissolution that even the senior German commanders lost

△ △ *The last stand . . .*
△ *. . . and the last* Heil.

touch with their crumbling front. O[ne?] day a German corps commander dr[ove] into a field of listless soldiers and ask[ed] why they were not fighting the Alli[es]. Not until an American MP clasped h[im] on the shoulder and invited him to j[oin] the throng, did the general learn that [he] had stumbled into a PW concentratio[n]

Altogether, the second phase of t[he] battle for the Rhineland, called Ope[ra]tion "Lumberjack", had brought t[he] 12th Army Group 51,000 prisoners. It h[ad] also given it the priceless bridgehead [at] Remagen, which the German 15th Ar[my] was unable to destroy, since the fo[ur] Panzer divisions which Model had giv[en]

A German soldier lies dead on the bank of the Rhine, the Third Reich's "uncrossable" natural defence in the West.

e energetic Lieutenant-General Bayer-
in for this purpose did not total more
an 5,000 men, 60 tanks, and 30 guns.
n the other side of the battlefield, the
mericans spread out in all directions.
o great and thorough was their push
at, on March 22, they were on the right
nk of the Rhine in a bridgehead 25 miles
ng and ten miles deep.

o retreat

s explained earlier, because of the forces
d *matériel* requested by Montgomery

in order to lead his army group across the
Rhine to the north of the Ruhr,
Eisenhower had at first limited his operation to the left bank of the Mosel. However, Hitler's obstinate decision to keep
his Army Group "G" inside the salient
limited by Haguenau, Saarbrücken,
Cochem (north of the Mosel), and
Koblenz, would convince him that the
best thing to do was to strike a third blow
at the enemy on the west of the Rhine,
which meant that the 3rd Army and the
6th Army Group would be able to take
part.

Colonel-General Hausser, commanding Army Group "G", had just been given

△ *An American artillery column streams past the wreckage of a German convoy blasted by the Allies' heavy guns.*

the 7th Army, recently taken over by General Obstfelder, and which was at present heavily engaged against Patton.

Hausser still had the 1st Army (General Foertsch), which was occupying the Moder front and the Siegfried Line or *Westwall* as far as the approaches to Forbach. The 19th Army, having evacuated the Colmar pocket, now came directly under the command of O.K.W. But at this time all these units totalled only 13 divisions, most of them badly worn, though some of them still gave a good account of themselves, for example the 2nd Mountain Division (Lieutenant-General Degen), and the 6th S.S. Mountain Division (Lieutenant-General Brenner).

Under these conditions, Hausser and his army commanders were of the opinion that they ought to put the Rhine, between the junctures of the Mosel and the Lauter,

behind them as soon as possible and ready to abandon the Siegfried Li after having destroyed all its install tions. But Hitler reacted indignant to this suggestion of destroying a maste piece of German military engineeri to which he had contributed so muc

The Führer was mistaken about t value of this construction, howeve Patton, who visited one of the fortress taken by the 76th Division, points out i weak point with his usual perspicacit

"It consisted of a three storey su merged barracks with toilets, show baths, a hospital, laundry, kitche store rooms and every conceivable co venience plus an enormous telepho installation. Electricity and heat we produced by a pair of identical dies engines with generators. Yet the who offensive capacity of this installatio nsisted of two machine guns and a 60-m mortar operating from steel cupolas which worked up and down by means of draulic lifts. The 60-mm mortar was culiar in that it was operated by remote ntrol. As in all cases, this particular l box was taken by a dynamite charge ainst the back door. We found marks the cupolas, which were ten inches ick, where our 90-mm shells fired at a nge of two hundred yards, had simply unced."

But neither Hitler nor his sub-dinates imagined that Patton would ed only four or five days to shift the ntre of gravity of his 3rd Army from ohl and Koblenz on the Rhine to Mayen the Nette and Cochem on the Mosel. the left, VIII Corps, now reduced to o divisions, would keep watch on blenz. In the centre, XII Corps, in-eased to six divisions (5th, 76th, 89th, d 90th Infantry, and 4th and 11th moured), was given Bingen on the ine and Bad-Kreuznach on the Nahe its first targets. On the right, XX rps with four divisions (26th, 80th, d 94th Infantry and 10th Armoured) d orders to press on to Kaiserslautern hind the backs of the defenders of the estwall, which would be attacked ntally by the American 7th Army. e latter, commanded by Lieutenant-neral Alexander M. Patch, had 12 visions, including the 3rd Algerian vision. As can be seen, the third act of e Battle of the Rhine, named "Under-ne" was about to match 22 more or less tact Allied divisions against 13 worn-t German ones. Actually, since the d of January, the 7th Army had been iting poised between Haguenau and rbach.

As for the 3rd Army, its losses, between nuary 29 and March 12, amounted to ly 21,581 officers, N.C.O.s, and men, which 3,650 had been killed and 1,374 re missing, which gives a daily divi-nal average of eight killed or missing d 32 wounded. These figures would ggest that despite his nickname of lood and Guts", Patton was not at all odigal with the lives of his men.

riumphant advance

n the evening of March 14, XII Corps d already got most of its 5th and 90th visions over on the right bank of the

Mosel at Treis, eight miles below Cochem. Eddy then wasted no time in unleashing his 4th and 11th Armoured Divisions.

To his right, XX Corps was attacking towards Saint Wendel, in the rear of the *Westwall*. At last, at dawn on March 15, H-hour came for the 7th Army. Its VI Corps (3rd Algerian, 36th, 42nd, and 103rd Divisions and 14th Armoured Division), went into the attack on the Moder front. Its 15th Division attacked the *Westwall*, its left towards Saarlautern, the French Sarrelouis, in contact with XX Corps.

By March 16, the 4th Armoured Division had advanced 32 miles in 48 hours. As it crossed the Nahe, near Bad-Kreuznach, it clashed violently with the 2nd Panzer Division (Major-General von Lauchert). But Patton was aware of the audacity of Gaffey, his ex-chief-of-staff, and had not let him fight it out alone. Opportunely reinforced, the 4th Armoured Division defeated the desperate counter-attack and moved forward again. By March 19, it had arrived seven miles west of Worms and 12 miles south-west of Mainz. On the same day, XX Corps, to which the 7th Army had given the 12th Armoured Division, under Major-General R. R. Allen, pushed its armoured spear-heads as far as 15 miles from Kaisers-lautern. Since the crossing of the Mosel, the 3rd Army had lost, including accidents, only 800 men, while it had taken 12,000 prisoners.

Forty-eight hours later, in XII Corps, the 90th Division, which had lost two commanders in Normandy, was busy mopping up Mainz, the 4th Armoured Division was occupying Worms, and the 11th was pushing on to the south of the city.

In XX Corps, Major-General Walton H. Walker had thrown his 12th Armoured Division into Ludwigshafen and was pushing his 10th towards Landau. Just as the difficult terrain of the Eifel had been no impediment, that of the Huns-ruck, which is just as bad, had not been able to hold back the *élan* of the 3rd Army, supported flexibly and efficiently by Major-General Otto P. Weyland's XIX Tactical Air Command of the 9th Air Force.

Facing the German 1st Army, the American 7th Army had had a consider-ably more difficult task. There is some evidence of this in a note made by Pierre Lyautey who, as liaison officer, was with the 3rd Algerian Division (General

△ *General Sir Miles Dempsey, commander of the British 2nd Army, on an inspection tour of his front line units.*

△ An American quadruple .5-inch A.A. mounting on a half-track chassis on watch against German aircraft near the Château de Vianden in Luxembourg.

Guillaume), when it attacked across the Moder.

"March 15: Artillery preparation. The planned 2,000 shells light up the scene. Attack by the 4th Tunisians. Skirmishes. The leading company runs, at seven in the morning, from ruin to ruin, lonely wall to lonely wall, reaches the railway, dives into the underground passage and jumps up into the mangled and dismantled gasworks. Violent reaction from German artillery, mortar, and machine guns. Impossible to move out. The whole sector is alive with fire. The company shelters in the gas-works. First one tank explodes, then another. Beyond the church, the scene is one of a major offensive: stretcher-bearers, stretchers, limping men walking around with white cards, a smell of blood, stifling heat. The last cows of Oberhoffen-Bénarès are in their death agony among the rubble."

It took four days for Major-General Edward H. Brooks, commanding VI Corps, to take back from the Germans the ground lost in lower Alsace as a result of Operation *"Nordwind"*. Then he closed in on the *Westwall* between the Rhine and the Vosges.

Both General de Gaulle and General de Lattre had no intention, however, of allowing the French Army to be restricted to a purely defensive function on the left bank of the Rhine. They wanted to see it play a part in the invasion of the Third Reich. While awaiting a definite decision

from S.H.A.E.F., General de Gaulle write "General Devers, a good ally and a go friend, sympathised with de Lattre wishes".

That is why, on March 18, General Monsabert received command of a ta force comprising the 3rd Algerian Div sion and two-thirds of the 5th Armour Division; aiming for Speyer, it wou give the French 1st Army a front over t Rhine in Germany.

The three infantry divisions of t United States VI Corps took three da and lost 2,200 men to overcome that pa of the *Westwall* allotted to them as obje tive, but using its infantry and enginee turn, Brooks finally pierced the defences between Wissembourg and Pirmasens. As for Monsabert, he had difficulty in front of the Bienwald. Nevertheless, his tanks were around Maximiliansau opposite Karlsruhe by the evening of March 24.

Patch had taken Landau the day before, so the Battle of the Palatinate, the third act of the Battle of the Rhine, was drawing to its end.

The battle had been conducted to Eisenhower's complete satisfaction. Between February 8 and March 24, the enemy had lost 280,000 prisoners, the remains of five German armies which had crossed back over the Rhine between the German-Dutch and Franco-German frontiers. Army Group "B" had suffered most. Patton alone could claim 140,112 prisoners, against the 53,000 taken by the 21st Army Group in Operation "Veritable/ Grenade". Therefore Eisenhower had proved his superiority not only over Hitler's arms but also over Montgomery's arguments.

Furthermore, on the night of March 22/23, Patton also succeeded in crossing the Rhine as Bradley had recommended, profiting from the Germans' disorder. The banks there being suitable, Patton chose the stretch near Oppenheim, which

△ *The great prize. Men and vehicles of the American 1st Army pour across the Ludendorff railway bridge over the Rhine at Remagen to establish an invincible bridgehead on the right bank.*

was occupied by the 5th Division (Major-
General S. LeRoy Irwin), half-way between Worms and Mainz.

Surprise crossing

At 2230 hours, 200 Piper L-4 Grass-
hoppers began to shuttle from one bank to
the other. These small observation and
artillery-spotting aircraft carried an
armed infantryman instead of an observer.
Once the first bridgehead had thus been
formed, the 12 L.C.V.P.s (Landing Craft
Vehicle/Personnel) of the "naval detachment" which Patton had trained to a
high pitch of efficiency on the Moselle
at Toul, entered the river while his bridging crews, from which he had refused to
be separated (lest he not get them back)
when he had driven hard from the
Sarre to the Ardennes, began to work
at once under the command of Brigadier-
General Conklin, the 3rd Army's chief
engineer.

At dawn on March 23, the 5th Division
had already placed six infantry battalions,
about 4,000 or 5,000 men, on the right bank
of the Rhine, at the cost of only eight
killed and 20 wounded. The Germans
were so surprised that when Patton made
his report to Bradley, he asked him not to
publicise the news, so as to keep the
Germans in the dark while they expected
him at the approaches to Mainz. As an
all-American soldier, he was happy to
have stolen a march over "Monty" by
forcing the Rhine before him and without
making any demands on anybody.

As a result, 48 hours later, five divisions
of the 3rd Army had crossed the Rhine at
Oppenheim, stretched along the valley
of the Main: XII Corps towards Aschaffenburg, and XX Corps towards Hanau.

Advance to the Rhine

Area occupied by January 31
Area occupied by March 24
Allied thrusts
Army group boundary
Army boundary
Siegfried Line (Westwall)

CHAPTER 147
Across the Rhine

n March 8, 1945, Field-Marshal Kessel-
ng was ordered to leave the Italian
eatre of operations immediately and
 to an audience with the *Führer*. The
llowing afternoon, Hitler told him that
 a result of the unfortunate situation
 Remagen, he had decided to make him
ommander-in-Chief in the West. In
 account of the meeting, Kesselring
ites:

"Without attaching any blame to Rundstedt, Hitler justified his action with
the argument that a younger and more
flexible leader, with greater experience
of fighting the Western powers, and still
possessing the troops' full confidence,
could perhaps make himself master of
the situation in the West. He was aware
of the inherent difficulties of assuming
command at such a juncture, but there

▽ *The Americans cross the
Rhine: an M24 Chaffee light tank
prepares to reverse into a landing
craft on the west bank prior to
going across, while other landing
craft shuttle to and fro in the
background and B-24 Liberator
bombers head east to disrupt
German communications
further.*

△ *Trucks fitted with special jigs move pontoons up towards the west bank of the Rhine in preparation for the American 9th Army's crossing.*

was no alternative but for me to make this sacrifice in spite of the poor state of my health. He had full confidence in me and expected me to do all that was humanly possible."

Such was the conclusion of the general review of the situation that Hitler had spent several hours discussing with Kesselring, first alone, later in the company of Keitel and Jodl. On the whole, Hitler was optimistic about the future. One might have suspected him of trying to mislead Kesselring as to the true situation were it not for his own unique capacity for self-deception. In any event, he appeared satisfied with the course of events on the Eastern Front.

Hitler certainly thought that a collapse in the East would be the end of the war, but he had provided for this eventuality and added, according to Kesselring's notes taken immediately after the audience: "our main military effort is

directed to the East. He [Hitler] envisag the decisive battle there, with comple confidence. And he expects the enemy main attack to be launched at Berlin

For this reason the 9th Army, whi was charged with the defence of the cit had been given priority consideratio Under the command of General T. Buss it had:

1. adequate infantry strength, togeth with Panzer and anti-tank force

2. standard artillery strength and mo than adequate anti-aircraft defence deployed in considerable depth und the best artillery commanders ava able;

3. excellent positions, with the best defences, especially water barrier on both sides of the main battle lin and

4. in its rear the strongest position of a Berlin, with its fortified perimeter an whole defensive organisation.

△ *Waiting for the big day:
Allied supplies under camouflage
by the side of a road leading to
the Rhine and the heart of
Germany.*

So there were grounds for assurance
that the Berlin front would not be broken;
similarly with Army Group "Centre",
on the borders of Silesia and Czechoslovakia, which had gained notable
successes. Its commander, Schörner,
assured Hitler that "with reinforcements
and sufficient supplies, he would repel
all enemy attacks launched at him".
As regards the situation on the Western
front, the heavy losses sustained by the
British, Americans, and French over
months of heavy fighting were a factor
that should be taken into account. Furthermore, in Hitler's opinion, "the Allies
could not dismiss the natural obstacles
covering the German Army's positions.
The Allied bridgehead at Remagen was
the danger point and it was urgent it
should be mopped up; but there too Hitler
was confident."

In these conditions, Kesselring's task
was to hold on long enough for the Eastern

Front armies to be brought up to strength,
so that O.K.W. could then despatch the
necessary reinforcements to the armies
in the West. Within a short while, the
deficiencies of the Luftwaffe, held to
blame for the failures of recent months,
would be forgotten and Grand-Admiral
Dönitz's new submarines would have
turned the tables in the Battle of the
Atlantic, bringing much needed relief
to the defence of the Third Reich.

Kesselring caught off balance

Thus armed with encouragement, Kesselring received his chief-of-staff's report
in the night of March 9-10 at the H.Q. at
Ziegenberg just vacated by Rundstedt.
General Westphal had been his chief-of-

The Canadian Ram Kangaroo armoured personnel carrier

Weight: 26 tons.
Crew: 2.
Load: 12 infantrymen.
Armament: one .3-inch Browning machine gun.
Armour: front 45-mm, nose, sides, rear, and decking 38-mm, and belly 25-mm.
Engine: one Wright Continental R-975 radial, 400-hp.
Speed: 25 mph.
Range: 145 miles.
Length: 19 feet.
Width: 9 feet 6 inches.
Height: 6 feet 1 inch.

aff during his time as supreme commander in Italy, and Kesselring had complete confidence in him.

The new commander must have been considerably shocked by the unembroidered account of the situation that he received. With 55 battle-worn divisions giving him, on average, a average of 63 fighting men for each mile of the front, it was his task to hold 85 full strength Allied divisions, which also enjoyed all the benefits of undisputed air superiority.

On March 11, at the H.Q. of LIII Corps, Kesselring met Field-Marshal Model and General von Zangen, commanding the 5th Army, which had been given the job of wiping out the Remagen bridgehead. All were agreed that this objective could not be attained unless there was considerable speeding up in the supply of substantial reinforcements, and above all of ammunition, and this filled Kesselring with apprehension. The morale of Army Group "H" gave him some comfort, however, especially since the enemy attack across the lower Rhine was taking time in getting under way. On the other hand, the position of Army Group "G", without any mobile reserves worthy of the name, seemed fraught with risk.

Hence Kesselring was not so much caught unawares as off guard by Operation "Undertone", which he learnt had been launched when he returned from this rapid tour of inspection. The cadence given the attack by Patton, Walker, Eddy, and their excellent divisional commanders was a disagreeable revelation to the Germans; Kesselring wrote:

"What clearly emerged was the rapid succession of operations (showing that the Allies had abandoned their Italian campaign strategy) as well as the competency of command and the almost reckless engagement of armoured units in terrain that was quite unsuited for the use of heavy tanks. On the basis of my experience in Italy in similar terrain, I was not expecting the American armoured forces to achieve rapid success, in spite of the fact that the reduced strength of tired German troops gave undoubted advantage to the enemy operation."

△ *Men of the Cheshire Regiment prepare to board the Landing Vehicles Tracked that will ferry them over the Rhine in the afternoon of March 24. At 2200 hours the previous night, the 1st Commando Brigade had made an assault landing on the east bank and secured the bridgehead into which the Cheshire Regiment moved as reinforcements.*
Overleaf: *White phosphorus shells from the U.S. 3rd Army's artillery rain down on the slopes above a small Rhenish town.*

In the face of this violent American thrust, O.B. West appealed to O.K.W. for authorisation to withdraw the German 1st and 7th Armies to the right bank of the Rhine; typically, Hitler procrastinated until it was too late to accept this eminently reasonable course. And the only reinforcement destined for the Western Front was a single division, which was not even combat-worthy as it had spent some considerable time in Denmark on garrison duties. To cap this, Kesselring was informed of the surprise attack at Oppenheim, while the 1st Parachute Army brought news that north of the Ruhr, smokescreens maintained over several hours showed that Montgomery was putting the final touches to his careful preparations.

To surrender or not?

It was in these circumstances that Kesselring was contacted by *Obergruppenführer* Karl Wolff of the *Waffen*-S.S., whom he had known in the capacity of "Plenipotentiary for the Wehrmacht in the rear of the Italian Front". For the past few weeks, this officer had been engaged, via Major Waibel of Swiss Army Intelligence, in negotiation with Allen Dulles, head of the American Secret Services in Berne, about terms for the capitulation of the German forces fighting in Italy. On March 23, Kesselring, who knew what Wolff was up to, saw him in his office in Ziegenberg, where Wolff suggested directly that the German armies in the West should be associated with this bid for surrender.

Kesselring refused, in spite of the succession of telephone calls informing him of the rapid progress made by the Americans, who had broken out of the Oppenheim bridgehead. According to Wolff's report to Dulles, Kesselring's opposition was based on both moral and practical arguments:

"He was defending soil and he was bound to continue even if he died himself in the fighting. He said he personally owed everything to the Führer, his rank, his appointment, his decorations. To this he added that he hardly knew the generals commanding the corps and divisions under him. Moreover, he had a couple of well-armed S.S. divisions behind him which he was certain would take action against him if he undertook anything

Field-Marshal Albrecht von Kesselring was born in Bavaria in 1885. He served as a staff officer in the artillery throughout World War I and the 1920's, and in 1933 he was transferred to the air force. He commanded the Luftwaffe in the German invasion of Poland and Belgium, and ordered the bombing of the B.E.F. as it evacuated Dunkirk. He conducted the extremely successful bombing raids on R.A.F. bases in southern England in 1940 and in July of that year he was made a Field-Marshal. In 1941 he was appointed C.-in-C., South, sharing with Rommel the command of the North African campaign and taking over during Rommel's absence and later during the retreat from Tunisia. In 1943 he was C.-in-C. in Italy, conducting a brilliant campaign despite the indifference of his superiors to his constant pleas for air reinforcements. For over a year he held out against the Allied advance, with a superbly conceived line of defences behind Cassino. In 1945 he succeeded the cream of Hitler's generals on the Western Front in a desperate attempt to check the Allied advance, but in March he had to surrender the southern half of the German forces to the Allies. He was sentenced to death by a British military court for executing Italian hostages, but in 1947 his sentence was commuted to life imprisonment and in 1952 he was released on the grounds of ill health. He died in 1960.

▷ *American paratroops dig in under the trees of a German orchard after the airborne landings just to the east of the Allied bridgeheads over the Rhine. The Germans, who had expected landings much further behind their lines, were caught entirely on the wrong foot by the Allied use of airborne troops in a tactical rather than a strategic rôle.*

▽ *The parachute drops begin in the Wesel area. This photograph was taken by Sergeant Fred W. Quandt of San Francisco, California, from a B-17 camera plane. The B-17 was shot down a few minutes later—the first aircraft casualty of the operation.*

The British General Aircraft Hamilcar I glider

Capacity: one Tetrarch or Locust light tank, or two Universal carriers, or 17,500 lbs of cargo.
Towing speed: 150 mph.
Weight empty/loaded: 18,500/36,000 lbs.
Span: 110 feet.
Length: 68 feet 1 inch.
Height: 20 feet 3 inches.
Crew: 2.

△ *A German N.C.O. illustrates
how to fire a Panzerfaust 30m
anti-tank rocket projector. There
were four Panzerfaust models,
all working the same way: the
rocket was contained in a tube
held under the arm or over the
shoulder. When fired, the rocket
motor drove the weapon out of
the tube and on towards the
target. Just as the weapon left
the tube, a cap at the latter's
rear was pushed off, allowing
the exhaust to fan out to the
rear. The warhead of the rocket
was a hollow-charge device
containing 3 pounds 7½ ounces of
explosive, capable of penetrating
200 mm of armour sloped at
30 degrees. It was an extremely
efficient weapon, with a punch
equal to that of the dual-purpose
8.8-cm gun.*

△▷ *German prisoners are
escorted through the town of
Hamminkeln by their captors,
men of the British 6th Airborne
Division.*

▽▷ *German civilians and
prisoners hug the ground in the
courtyard of a captured
farmhouse in an effort to protect
themselves from retaliatory
German artillery fire.*

against the Führer's orders."

Nevertheless Kesselring had no objection to a German capitulation in Italy, and the *Obergruppenführer* was quite free to convey to the former's successor, Colonel-General von Vietinghoff, that O.B. West entirely approved the project.

Scorched earth policy

Whatever one may think of the ethical considerations behind Kesselring's refusal, he understandably felt no scruples in giving his support to Albert Speer, Reich Minister for Armaments and War Production, who was doing all he could to sabotage the execution of the "scorched earth" order promulgated by Hitler on March 19, 1945.

In setting out its motives, the monstrous *Führerbefehl* used the following line of argument:

"The fight for the existence of our people obliges us to make total use, even within the Reich, of whatever means may weaken the fighting power of the enemy and prevent him from pursuing his advance. Any means capable, directly or indirectly, of inflicting lasting damage on the offensive strength of the enemy must be resorted to. It is erroneous to think that by leaving them intact or with only superficial damage, we may more profitably resume exploitation of our communication and transport systems and our industrial or productive installations when we reconquer our invaded territory. When the enemy comes to retreat, he will have no consideration for the population, and will leave only scorched earth behind him.

"For this reason I command:

1. that within the Reich the communications and military transport systems, and the industrial and productive installations, which the enemy may use immediately or within a limited period for the prosecution of the war, be destroyed."

Article 2 of the same decree divided powers for this purpose between the military chiefs and the civil administrators; and Article 3, ordering the immediate transmission of the order to army commanders, declared invalid any directive which sought to nullify it.

So Hitler joined Morgenthau, whereas even Churchill and Roosevelt had rejected the inhuman and demented notion of "pastoralising" the German peopl Albert Speer, however, devoted his entir energies to opposing the implementatio of this insane order: verbally on Marc 18; and in writing in two letters, th second of which, dated March 29, i preserved among the appendices tha Percy Ernst Schramm adds as a suppl ment to his masterly edition of the O.K.W war diary. The extract chosen below evidence enough for the reader that th motives which inspired Hitler on thi occasion were essentially the same those of the Scythian kings who, o their deathbeds, according to Herodotu caused their favourite wives, their se vants, and even their horses to b sacrificed. And, Speer wrote:

"From what you have told me th evening [March 18] the following emerge clearly and unequivocally, unless I hav misunderstood you: if we are to lose th war, the German people are to be lost a well. This destiny is unavoidable. Th being so, it is not necessary to secure th basic conditions to enable our people t ensure their own survival even in th most primitive form. Rather, on th contrary, we should ourselves destro them. For they will have proved them selves the weaker, and the future wi belong exclusively to the people of th east, who will have shown themselves th stronger. Furthermore, only th unworthy will survive since the best an bravest will have fallen."

Speer did not limit his oppositio merely to pious utterances. He put th enormous weight of influence he had a dictator of industrial production to th task of avoiding implementation of th "scorched earth" order.

In this covert activity he receive positive support from Kesselring; as result, in its retreat from the Rhine t the Elbe and beyond, the German Arm restricted itself to forms of destructio which are common in such cases to a the armies in the world. Two circun stances favoured Speer in carrying ou his policy: the headlong nature of th Allied advance after March 31 and, i the German camp, the explosives crisi further exacerbated by the disorganisa tion of transport.

At the end of 1966, on his release fro Spandau prison, to which he had bee sent by the Nuremberg trial, Albert Spee was greeted by manifestations of syn pathy. This was interpreted by som as the sign they had been seeking sinc

45 of a recrudescence of Nazism in the
Federal Republic. Such an interpretation
seems quite unwarranted. Rather, it
would seem that Speer's sympathisers
wanted to show public recognition of the
man who, in spite of Hitler and at the
risk of his life, had chosen to safeguard
the means of survival and recovery so
that one day another Germany might
live.

Montgomery prepares to cross the Rhine

On March 23, at 1530 hours, under a clear
sky and with a favourable weather forecast, Montgomery launched Operation
"Plunder/Varsity" and addressed the
American, British, and Canadian troops
under his command with an order of the
day which concluded with these words:
"6. 21 ARMY GROUP WILL NOW

The American Landing Vehicle Tracked (L.V.T.) 2 Buffalo

Weight: $14\frac{3}{4}$ tons.
Crew: 2 to 7.
Armament: one .5-inch M2 and one .3-inch M1919A4 machine gun.
Engine: one Continental W670-9A radial, 250-hp.
Speed: 20 mph on land and $7\frac{1}{2}$ mph in water.
Range: 150 miles on land and 100 miles in water.
Length: 26 feet 2 inches.
Width: 10 feet 8 inches.
Height: 8 feet $2\frac{1}{2}$ inches.

CROSS THE RHINE

The enemy possibly thinks he is safe behind this great river obstacle. We all agree that it is a great obstacle; but we will show the enemy that he is far from safe behind it. This great Allied fighting machine, composed of integrated land and air forces, will deal with the problem in no uncertain manner.

7. And having crossed the Rhine, we will crack about in the plains of Northern Germany, chasing the enemy from pillar to post. The swifter and the more energetic our action, the sooner the war will be over, and that is what we all desire; to get on with the job and finish off the German war as soon as possible.

8. Over the Rhine, then, let us go. And good hunting to you all on the other side.

9. May 'The Lord mighty in battle' give us the victory in this our latest undertaking, as He has done in all our battles since we landed in Normandy on D-Day."

The Rhine, which in 21st Army Group's sector is about 400 yards wide and has a current of about six feet per second, was

the "great obstacle" of which Montgomery spoke. But the means given him to cross it were also great.

Under his command he had two armies, eight corps, and 27 divisions (17 infantry, eight armoured, and two airborne; or, in national terms, 13 American, 12 British, and two Canadian). To these should be added the equivalent of three divisions represented by five armoured brigades, a British commando brigade, and the Canadian 9th Infantry Brigade.

The British 2nd Army's attack, supplemented by the Canadian II Corps, was prepared for and supported by 1,300 pieces of artillery, with 600 guns fulfilling the same function for XVI Corps, which was to open the right bank of the Rhine for the American 9th Army. Such concentration of firepower necessitated the transport and dumping of 60,000 tons of ammunition. Massive area bombing by the Allied air forces extended the artillery action to the Germans' rear areas, thus isolating the battlefield. Between March 20 and 22, R.A.F. Bomber Command and the U.S. 8th and 9th Air Forces made 16,000 sorties over the area in question and dropped 49,500 tons of bombs (including 22,000-lb "Grand

△ *A battery of British 40-mm Bofors guns in action in the direct support rôle.*
Overleaf: *An American Landing Vehicle Tracked (L.V.T.) splashes into the Rhine under cover of a thick smokescreen.*

Slams").

To build bridges across the Rhine, 30,000 tons of engineering equipment and 59,000 engineers had to be transported to the area. But before the construction required by Operation "Plunder" could be used, divisions in the first line of attack had to be conveyed from one bank to the other by other means. This task was carried out by a detachment of the Royal Navy, which left Antwerp to reach its departure point by a series of Belgian, Dutch, and German canals. With Vice-Admiral Sir Harold M. Burrough in overall command, it comprised 45 landing craft (L.C.M.), plus a formation of the 12-ton amphibious tanks known by the British as Buffaloes and as Alligators by the Americans. Preparations on this scale were obviously observable by the enemy, but the final deployment of the Allied forces was conceal by the smokescreen which hid the l bank of the Rhine over a distance of miles between dawn on March 21 a 1700 hours on March 23.

As is apparent, Montgomery had on more showed his immense capacity f organisation. In the course of the batt which followed, he would confirm h reputation as an exceptional tactici by winning back for himself the advanta of surprise which he had lost as a resu of such tremendous concentration forces. And, it should be noted, the are few men who, like him, combi such attention to detail in preparatic with such vigour of execution.

On the right bank of the Rhine, the 1 Parachute Army was deployed with right slightly upstream of Emmeri and its left in the region of Duisburg.

as thus defending a front of 45 miles with seven divisions, an adequate concentration for defence, bearing in mind the natural obstacle of the broad river, had the divisions been at full complement. During the relative lull following March 11, they had dug themselves in well and the rapid construction of their defensive positions was entirely satisfactory to Kesselring. General Schlemm had played a considerable rôle here; Major Milton Shulman, of the Canadian 1st Army, had the opportunity of interrogating him later, and writes:

"His record, coupled with an orderly mind and a keen grasp of tactical problems, placed him amongst the more able generals still available in the Wehrmacht."

However, faced by Montgomery's eight divisions and five armoured brigades, Schlemm's only mobile reserves were the 116th Panzer and 15th *Panzergrenadier* Divisions, of XLVII Panzer Corps, which he had put in reserve behind his centre. At a higher command level, in Army Group "H", Colonel-General Blaskowitz was similarly short of men, and the meagre reserves found by Kesselring were spent in containing the twin thrust of the American 1st Army bursting out of the Remagen bridgehead, and the 3rd Army exploiting at record speed the bridgeheads it had won at Hanau and Aschaffenburg on the Main.

O.K.W. and O.B. West confidently expected an airborne landing. Accordingly, an entire anti-aircraft corps was put at the disposal of Blaskowitz, who deployed batteries all over the area between Munster and the right bank of the Rhine. But apparently to little effect:

△ *The disillusionment of defeat on the face of a 16-year old captured by the Americans.*
▷ *U.S. troops move off towards the front after crossing the Rhine.*

as on previous occasions the German soldier had to put up with implacable and practically unchallenged machine gun and cannon fire and bombing from Allied aircraft without seeing any fighters of his own in the sky.

The battle begins

At 1700 hours on March 23, the smoke-screen vanished and the entire artillery of the British 2nd Army and the American 9th Army opened fire on the enemy positions, maintaining their barrage of shells of all calibres until 0945 hours the following morning. This was, however, interspersed with pauses at times varying from sector to sector to allow the divisions launching the attack to feel out the enemy strength.

The main action devolved upon the British 2nd Army, in position north of the Lippe. On its left, XXX Corps had during the night got four battalions of the 51st Division (Major-General Thomas Rennie) across the Rhine; on its right, XII Corps had established its 15th Division (Major-General Colin Muir Barber) on the right bank of the river, opposite Xanten, while the 1st Commando Brigade went into action against the 180th Division in the ruins of Wesel. Further south, the American 9th Army, whose task was to cover the flank of the British attack, engaged its XVI Corps, whose 30th and 79th Divisions crossed the Rhine to either side of Rheinberg. According to Montgomery, German resistance was only sporadic, and certainly the two American divisions mentioned above suffered only 31 killed in the enterprise.

The offensive undertaken by the 21st Army Group was no surprise for Blaskowitz, who had even correctly estimated its main point of impact and line of advance. Accordingly—and with a degree of haste for which Kesselring reproached him—he judged it opportune to throw in his armoured reserves. The dawn saw furious counter-attacks which drew the following observation from Sir Brian Horrocks, then in command of XXX Corps:

"Reports were coming in of Germans surrendering in large numbers to the British and American forces on our flanks but there was no sign of any collapse on our front. In fact the 51st Highland Division reported that the

enemy was fighting harder than at a time since Normandy. It says a lot for morale of those German parachute a panzer troops that with chaos, organisation and disillusionment around them they should still be res ing so stubbornly."

In the course of the fighting betwe XXX Corps and the 15th *Panzergrenad* Division, which brought into the line paratroops from the German 6th and Parachute Divisions, Major-Gene Rennie was killed, evidence enough the enemy's determination.

Airborne landings

However, at 1000 hours the "event", the Napoleonic sense of the word, to place. In the German camp, remember the precedent of Arnhem, the Alli airborne troops were expected to atta at the time that Montgomery's infan was attempting to cross the Rhine, and drop to the rear of the battlefield to eff a vertical encirclement of the 1st Pa chute Army. But their attack came th hours after it had been anticipated, a the drop took place in the region of Ha minkeln, barely five miles from the ri bank of the river. Under the comma of Lieutenant-General Matthew B. Ri way, XVIII Airborne Corps compri the British 6th Airborne (Major-Gene E. Bols) and the American 17th Airbo (Major-General William E. Miley) Di sions, their transport being undertak by 1,572 planes and 1,326 gliders, un close escort from 889 fighters. The Airborne Division took off from 11 fields in the south-east of England, American 17th from 17 that had just b built in the area bounded by Rhei Orléans, Evreux, and Amiens. The eff of surprise was so great and the Germ *flak* so well neutralised by Allied artill pounding from the left bank that losses landing amounted to no more than transport planes and three per cent of glider force employed in this operati known as "Varsity".

The British and Americans fell on enemy battery positions and reduced good many of them to silence, then thr on across the Diersforterwald to m XII Corps, whose advance was stron supported by 580 heavy guns of the 2 Army, responding to calls for fire co with most admirable speed and precisi

the end of the day, XVIII Airborne
rps made contact with the British
I Corps. Furthermore, thanks to units
wn in by glider, XVIII Airborne Corps
d taken intact a number of bridges over
e IJssel which, flowing as it does parallel
the Rhine between Wesel and Em-
rich, could have constituted an obstacle
the rapid exploitation of the day's
ccesses. Moreover, the 84th Division
s taken in rear and as good as
nihilated, with the loss of most of the
'89 prisoners counted by General Ridg-
y's Intelligence services.

arge bridgehead

night fell, in the zone between Din-
ken and Rees, where resistance from
rman parachute troops had lost none
its spirit, the 21st Army Group had
ken a bridgehead 30 miles wide on the
ht bank of the Rhine, running, in the
itish XII Corps' (Lieutenant-General
Neil Methuen Ritchie) sector to a
pth of nearly eight miles; the Allied
idge builders were free to get to work
thout any threat of retaliation on the
rt of enemy artillery. Montgomery
uld feel all the more satisfaction with
e way things had gone on March 24 as
had committed only four of his eight
rps.

isenhower's
xcellent plan

om an observation post situated a mile
so south of Xanten, which commanded
good view over the vast Westphalian
ain, Churchill, together with Brooke
d Eisenhower, saw the British and
merican XVIII Airborne Corps' trans-
rt planes cross overhead and return,
t missed the drop itself because of the
st. As the success of the operation
came apparent, General Eisenhower
ports that Field-Marshal Brooke turned
him and said:
"Thank God, Ike, you stuck by your
an. You were completely right, and I am
rry if my fear of dispersed effort added
your burdens. The German is now
ked. It is merely a question of when he
ooses to quit. Thank God, you stuck by
ur guns.''

◁ American infantry
..bark on an L.C.V.(P.) to
..ss the Rhine.
◁ Men of the U.S. 7th Army
..pare to cross south of Worms
..utboard engine-powered
..uck" craft.
..haffee light tanks of the U.S.
.. Army and their transport.
..roops of the 7th Army
..bark during the morning of
..rch 26.
..A pensive moment just before
.. landings for infantry of the
.. Army.

The American M22 Locust air-transportable light tank

Weight: 7.4 tons.
Crew: 3.
Armament: one 37-mm M6 gun with 50 rounds and one .3-inch Browning machine gun with 2,500 rounds.
Armour: hull lower front 25-mm, upper front, lower sides, rear, and belly 13-mm, upper sides and decking 9-mm; turret 25-mm.
Engine: one Lycoming O-435T inline, 162-hp.
Speed: 40 mph on roads and 30 mph cross-country.
Range: 135 miles on roads.
Length: 12 feet 11 inches.
Width: 7 feet 4½ inches.
Height: 4 feet 1 inch.

Coming across this passage in *Crusade Europe,* Lord Alanbrooke refers to entry in his diary made at the close of at same March 24, claiming that Eisenhower's remarks resulted from a misunderstanding, and that he had not in fact "seen the light" that day near unten. He wrote in 1949:

"To the best of my memory I congratulated him heartily on his success and said at, as matters had turned out, his policy was now the correct one; that, with the German in his defeated condition, no ngers now existed in a dispersal of ort."

Thus Brooke corrects the remark attributed to him (on this occasion) by Eisenhower. Obviously there is a difference between the two versions. Nevertheless, does not necessarily follow that Eisenhower was mistaken in defending his strategic plans, unless it can be shown that the German armies would have fallen into the state of ruin and confusion noted by Brooke that March 25 evening had not Operations "Lumberjack" and "Undertone" taken place.

Kesselring settles that question with greater authority than we can possibly claim to when he writes:

"Just as Remagen became the tomb of my Group 'B', the Oppenheim bridgehead seemed destined to become that of my Group 'G'. There too, the initial cket became a deep chasm, and devoured all the strength of the other parts the front, that somehow or other had been rendered mobile, as well as all the units brought up from the rear to fill the ps."

---

ollapse of the German 5th Army

March 25 and 28, two further events of mparable scale and importance took ace on the 12th Army Group's front: stly, the collapse of the German 15th Army, whose task it was to contain the enemy within the Remagen bridgehead; and secondly, adding its effect to the clean breakthrough by the American 1st Army, the crossing of the Main at the chaffenburg and Hanau bridges by the American 3rd Army. This manoeuvre lowed from a carefully prepared plan General Bradley's after the launching Operation "Lumberjack", which was

△ *Supplies for the 9th Army arrive by D.U.K.W. and jeep on the east bank of the Rhine.*

given its final touches following the surprise assault on Remagen. He describes it as follows in *A Soldier's Story:*

"Now that Hodges had established the Remagen bridgehead to the south of Bonn, he was to trace that original pattern. First he would speed his tanks down the autobahn where it ran through Limburg on the road to Frankfurt. At Limburg he was to turn east up the Lahn Valley to Giessen. There he would join Patton's pincer coming up from the Main.

"The First and Third Armies would then advance abreast of one another in a parallel column with Hodges on the inside, Patton on his flank, up the broad Wetteran corridor toward a union with Simpson. Then while Hodges and Simpson locked themselves around the Ruhr preparatory to cleaning it out, Patton would face his Army to the east and be prepared to advance toward the oncoming Russians."

So it was, but according to Kesselring, the execution of Bradley's plan was considerably eased by Model's preconceived ideas of the enemy's intentions. The commander of Army Group "B" was obsessed with his right flank, fearing an attack down the eastern bank of the Rhine aimed at an assault on the Ruhr industrial complex from the south; and he was deaf to all telephone calls from his superior, remonstrating with him for leaving his centre thinly protected.

On March 25, the American 1st Army

△ Sherman tanks roll into the ruins of Munster on April 3.

proved Kesselring's case by smashing LXXIV Corps in the region of Breitscheid. Hodges immediately unleashed his 3rd, 7th, and 9th Armoured Divisions, which reached Giessen and Marburg on the 28th, 53 and 66 miles respectively from the Rhine at Neuwied. On the same day, in the 3rd Army, VIII Corps completed the mopping up of Frankfurt and made contact with Hodges's right in the region of Wiesbaden, thus trapping the enemy elements left on the right bank of the Rhine between the Lahn and the Main. But most strikingly, Patton's 4th, 6th, and 11th Armoured Divisions, in formation ahead of XII and XX Corps, had moved from the Main valley into that of

the Fulda, making in the direction Kassel. Thus Hodges, whose task was reach the eastern outlets of the Ru basin, found himself provided with cov just as Bradley intended, against a cou ter-attack striking from the Harz mou tains.

The Ruhr pocket

On the day after the surpr breakthrough at Oppenheim, Kesselri according to his own account, h wondered "whether it was not best accept the army groups' proposals a the front, even if it were only to enable points in the rear to be mopped up or stray troops to be rounded up."

Quite clearly, at the point reached in the German camp on March 28, Kesselring's conclusions were still more justified.

This was all the more true as the sappers of the 21st Army Group had by March 26 opened seven 40-ton bridges to traffic, and the American 9th Army and British 2nd Army came down both banks of the Lippe to overwhelm the 1st Parachute Army. Two days later, on the left bank of this river, Lieutenant-General Simpson had his 8th Armoured Division (Major-General J. M. Devine) in the region of Haltern, more than 25 miles east of the Rhine. At the same time, Sir Miles Dempsey pushed the Guards Armoured Division (Major-General Allan Adair) down the Münster road, while his XXX and Canadian II Corps, on a line linking Borken – Bocholt – Isselburg – Emmerich, reached the Dutch frontier. The 1st Parachute Army was helplessly cut off, and its LXIII Corps and XLVII Panzer Corps (five divisions) were thrown back onto Army Group "B". And Montgomery poured his armoured units resolutely into the breach.

On April 2, 1945, as the day closed, the inevitable happened. The American 3rd Armoured Division, driving ahead of VII Corps (1st Army), met up at Lippstadt with the 8th Armoured Division coming from Haltern. In the course of this fighting, Major-General Rose, commanding the 3rd Armoured Division in its finest foray, was killed. Now Army Group "B" was encircled, with the exception of LXVII Corps, which had been attached to Army Group "B" following the breakthrough at Breitscheid.

Including the ruins of the 1st Parachute Army mentioned above, there were the 5th *Panzerarmee* and the 15th Army, of seven corps or 19 divisions (three of them Panzer, and the 3rd *Panzergrenadier* Division) caught in a trap that Hitler was quick to qualify as "the fortified region of the Ruhr". To reduce it, General Bradley formed a new 15th Army, under the command of Lieutenant-General Leonard T. Gerow, with a strength of five corps, including the newly-formed XXII and XXIII Corps, in all 18 divisions taken from the 1st and 9th Armies.

The encirclement of the Ruhr meant not only the rapid destruction of Army Group "B", but more importantly, the end of all organised resistance on the

hdraw the entire front from the Rhine. nally refrained from doing so, because only result would have been to re-at in disorder. Our troops were heavily en, barely mobile, in large part battle-ary, and encumbered by units in the r which were still in a state of dis-ler. The enemy had all-round superior-, especially in mobility and in the air. iothing occurred to check or slow his vance, our retreating columns would be rtaken and smashed. This type of com-would have become an end in itself-longer a means employed to an end-end being to gain time. Every day on Rhine, on the contrary, was a day ned, signifying a strengthening of

△ *Ulm Cathedral, surprisingly undamaged amidst the debris of the rest of the city.*

part of the Wehrmacht between Würzburg on the Main and Minden on the Weser. Between the inside of the wings of Army Groups "G" and "H", a breach of more than 180 miles was opened. It was too late for the unfortunate Kesselring to cherish the notion of repositioning his armies on a line along the courses of the Weser, Werra, Main, Altmuhl, and Lech, as favoured by 18th Century strategists.

Eisenhower gives up the idea of Berlin . . .

To stop this breach, O.K.W. still had, in the Harz mountains, the 11th Army, comprising five divisions under the command of General Wenck, and a 12th Army being formed on the right bank of the Elbe. But clearly the way to Berlin lay open to the 12th Army Group and on April 4 S.H.A.E.F. reinforced it with the American 9th Army, to the great satisfaction of General Simpson, its commander, and even more so of General Bradley, who saw the forces under his command now rise to four armies (11 corps of 48 divisions, 14 of them armoured, with some 3,600 tanks). But Eisenhower had no intention of giving Bradley the German capital as an objective. The question had already been considered by him among other options open to him after the encirclement of the Ruhr, and he had decided against going for Berlin for strategic and logistic reasons – in particular the lengthening of his lines of communication that this would entail, and the obstacle of the Elbe, something short of 200 miles from the Rhine and 125 from Berlin.

As a result of this decision, Eisenhower set himself the following objectives:
1. to make contact without delay with the Soviet forces moving west, and thus make it impossible for the enemy to try to regroup;
2. to hurl the 21st Army Group to the north-east, its right wing keeping its objective steadily fixed on Lübeck, to cut off the Wehrmacht forces occupying Norway and Denmark; and
3. for the 12th and 6th Army Groups, Eisenhower writes:

"Equally important was the desirability of penetrating and destroying the so-called 'National Redoubt'. For many weeks we had been receiving reports that the Nazi intention, in extremity, was [to] withdraw the cream of the S.S., Gesta[po] and other organisations fanatically [de]voted to Hitler, into the mountains [of] southern Bavaria, western Austria, a[nd] northern Italy. There they expected [to] block the tortuous mountain passes a[nd] to hold out indefinitely against the Alli[es]. Such a stronghold could always be [re]duced by eventual starvation if in [no] other way. But if the German was p[er]mitted to establish the redoubt he mi[ght] possibly force us to engage in a lo[ng] drawn-out guerrilla type of warfare, o[r] costly siege. Thus he could keep alive [a] desperate hope that through disagr[ee]ment among the Allies he might yet [be] able to secure terms more favoura[ble] than those of unconditional surrend[er]. The evidence was clear that the N[azi] intended to make the attempt and [we] decided to give him no opportunity [to] carry it out."

So, with the Elbe reached in the vicin[ity] of Magdeburg, it was understood t[hat] Bradley would make his main line [of] advance along a line Erfurt–Leipzi[g–] Dresden, with a secondary thrust [on] Regensburg and Linz. Contact would [be] made with the Russians in Saxony, a[nd] at the same time a march would be sto[len] on Army Group "G" in its task of occu[py]ing the redoubt. However logical t[his] line of argument was from a strate[gic] point of view, it rested on a hypothe[sis] which was shown to be false after G[er]many's capitulation: the "national [re]doubt" concept was no more than [a] figment of the imagination of those w[ho] fed it to S.H.A.E.F.'s Intellige[nce] services.

Stalin approves warmly . .

In any event, on March 24, in accordan[ce] with a decision taken at the Yalta C[on]ference, Eisenhower communicated [his] plan, summarised above, to Stalin w[ho] approved it most warmly. In the terms [of] a telegram cited in Churchill's memo[irs] but absent from *Crusade in Euro[pe]*, Stalin assured Eisenhower that his pl[an] "entirely coincides with the plan of t[he] Soviet High Command . . . Berlin has l[ost] its former strategic importance. T[he] Soviet High Command therefore pl[ans] to allot secondary forces in the directi[on] of Berlin." Knowing as we do that at t[his] very moment these lines were dictat[ed]

▽ A huge column of German prisoners wends its way back towards the American rear along one of the Autobahns *constructed by the Nazis to move troops and equipment swiftly – but with a different aim in mind.*

...alin was concentrating five tank armies ...d 25,000 guns (expending 25,600 tons ...shell) on an allegedly secondary objec- ...e, one sees what was in the wind.

.. but Churchill objects ..olently

...e plan elaborated by S.H.A.E.F. found ...strongest opponent in Churchill. Em- ...dying as he did the ancient traditions ...ich had inspired British diplomacy ...ce the reign of Henry VIII, he held as a ...xim that "as a war waged by a coalition ...aws to its end political aspects have a ...ounting importance."

...So it seemed obvious to him that since ...e military collapse of the Third Reich ...s a matter of only a few weeks, the ...ne had come for the two great Anglo- ...xon powers quietly to dismiss purely ...rategic considerations and consider political issues while there was still time. And in this field he was forced to admit that Stalin and Molotov viewed the Yalta agreement about Poland as being worth no more than the paper it was written on, and were set in their determination to allow no régime in Warsaw that was not subservient to Moscow.

Likewise, on March 2, Vishinsky, Soviet Deputy Minister of Foreign Affairs, in the course of a scene of abomin- able violence, had imposed a government chosen by the Kremlin on King Michael of Rumania. The ten per cent minority voice that Churchill had reserved in that country had fallen to all but nothing, and things were worse still in Bulgaria.

Hence Churchill thought that future operations conducted by S.H.A.E.F. should take account of political as well as military considerations, and these he enumerated and summarised as follows:

"*First,* that Soviet Russia had become a mortal danger to the free world.

▽ *American armour rumbles through the streets of Mönchengladbach in the Ruhr industrial area.*

Lt.-Gen. Sir Miles Dempsey was born in 1896 and first came to prominence at the head of XIII Corps in the Sicilian and Italian campaigns. Before the Normandy landings he was promoted to command the 2nd Army, which he then led up to the end of the war, winning a considerable reputation for committing his men to major actions only when he was convinced that success was almost certain.

Lt.-Gen. Henry Crerar was born in 1888 and served with the Canadian artillery in World War I. From 1935 to 1938 he was Director of Military Operations and Intelligence. He was Chief-of-Staff of the Canadian Army in 1940. He commanded the Canadian I Corps and later the 1st Army in Europe.

Secondly, that a new front must be immediately created against her onward sweep.

Thirdly, that this front in Europe should be as far east as possible.

Fourthly, that Berlin was the prime and true objective of the Anglo-American armies.

Fifthly, that the liberation of Czechoslovakia and the entry into Prague of American troops was of high consequence.

Sixthly, that Vienna, and indeed Austria, must be regulated by the Western Powers, at least upon an equality with the Russian Soviets.

Seventhly, that Marshal Tito's aggressive pretensions against Italy must be curbed.

Finally, and above all, that a settlement must be reached on all major issues between the West and the East *before the armies of democracy melted,* or the Western Allies yielded any part of the German territories they had conquered, or, as it could soon be written, liberated from totalitarian tyranny."

Eisenhower's plan therefore displeased him all the more because in communicating his intentions to Stalin, the Supreme Allied Commander appeared to have exceeded the commonly accepted limits of competence of a military chief; a somewhat dubious argument since Stalin had concentrated in himself the functions of head of government and generalissimo of the Soviet armed forces, in which capacity the communication had been addressed to him. With the approval of the British Chief-of-Staffs Committee and of Montgomery, the Prime Minister endeavoured to persuade Eisenhower to go back on his decision, and on April 1 an appeal was made to President Roosevelt, Field-Marshal Brooke making a similar appeal to General Marshall.

Eisenhower refuses to countermand his orders

But Eisenhower refused to give in. On March 31, when giving his instructions to Montgomery, he pointedly wrote:

"You will note that in none of this do I mention Berlin. That place has become, so far as I am concerned, nothing but a geographical location, and I have never been interested in these. My purpose is to destroy the enemy's forces and powers to resist."

On the next day Eisenhower receive[d] telegram from the American Joint Chie[fs] of-Staff, telling him that despite t[he] objections of the British chiefs, th[ey] supported him entirely, and that, [in] particular, the communication of [his] future plans to Stalin seemed to th[em] "to be a necessity dictated by operation[s]. Marshall concluded with the followi[ng] point to his allies:

"To deliberately turn away from t[he] exploitation of the enemy's weakne[ss] does not appear sound. The single obj[ec]tive should be quick and complete victo[ry]. While recognising there are factors [not] of direct concern to S.C.A.E.F., the U[.S.] chiefs consider his strategic concept [is] sound and should receive full support. [He] should continue to communicate free[ly] with the Commander-in-Chief of t[he] Soviet Army."

In his memoirs, Montgomery, wh[en] dealing with this difference of opini[on] quotes from a letter on the subject writt[en] to him by Eisenhower on September [4] of the previous year:

"Clearly, Berlin is the main pri[ze]. There is no doubt whatsoever, in [my] mind, that we should concentrate all o[ur] energies and resources on a rapid thru[st] to Berlin."

"But now he did not agree," ad[ds] Montgomery.

Nonetheless, the situation had to so[me] extent changed between September [and]

)44, and the close of March 1945. In articular, the Russians had moved forard from the Vistula to the Oder, and H.A.E.F. believed that Hitler and his rincipal collaborators were preparing o abandon Berlin and make for the leged "national redoubt". Hence the eich capital would seem to have lost onsiderably in value as an objective. One might be justified in concluding om this that in disregarding Berlin s the proper objective, Eisenhower, far om showing proof of versatility, was mply applying with some obtuseness e teaching he had absorbed at West oint: namely that the first and foremost bjective of any strategy worthy of the ame consists in destroying the forces of e enemy, and that a great general should ver subordinate this to geographical bjectives, however commanding they ppear. Marshall, too, had been trained the same principles. Added to this, th men were the less inclined to heed e advice of Brooke and Montgomery, hose criticism of the "broad front" d the dual attack on the Rhine had been validated by the course of recent ents.

An order from Roosevelt, in his capaty as head of the American armed forces, uld most certainly have led them to view their point of view purely and mply as military leaders. But no such der came. Here Roosevelt stuck to his principle of not intervening in matters of strategy; but even had he desired to do so, his health had now deteriorated to such an extent that he was no longer capable of making such decisions. According to Churchill, the Western powers found themselves in "the deadly hiatus which existed between the fading of President Roosevelt's strength and the growth of President Truman's grip of the vast world problem. In this melancholy void one President could not act and the other could not know. Neither the military chiefs nor the State Department received the guidance they required. The former confined themselves to their professional sphere; the latter did not comprehend the issues involved."

The facts could scarcely be better put. But it should not go unsaid that in his appeal to Roosevelt, Churchill was understandably less trenchant than later in his memoirs, with the world for his audience; he based his case for the occupation of Berlin on the following hypothesis:

"The Russian armies will no doubt overrun all Austria and enter Vienna. If they also take Berlin will not their impression that they have been the overwhelming contributor to our common victory be unduly imprinted in their minds, and may this not lead them into a mood which will raise grave and formidable difficulties in the future?"

Advance into Germany

NORTH SEA

GERMANY

HOLLAND

BELGIUM

LUXEMBOURG

FRANCE

SWITZERLAND

ITALY

CZECHOSLOVAKIA

AUSTRIA

YUGOSLAVIA

BAVARIA

Places labelled on map:
Eckernförde, Kiel, Neumünster, Cuxhaven, Lübeck, Wismar, Rostock, Stettin, Wilhelmshaven, Bremerhaven, Hamburg, Lüneburg, Wittenberge, Groningen, Assen, Meppel, Almelo, Deventer, Zutphen, Lingen, Minden, Hannover, Brunswick, Berlin, Amsterdam, Emmerich, Kleve, Münster, Magdeburg, Dessau, Wittenberg, Wesel, Lippe, Nordhausen, Eisleben, Halle, Torgau, Duisburg, Wuppertal, Kassel, Mündem, Mühlhausen, Leipzig, Cologne, Bonn, Marburg, Erfurt, Naumberg, Chemnitz, Remagen, Giessen, Fulda, Jena, Koblenz, Saafeld, Plauen, Ascheffenburg, Schweinfurt, Karlovy Vary, Oppenheim, Würzburg, Bamberg, Bayreuth, Plzeň, Worms, Michelstadt, Ludwigshafen, Nuremberg, České Budějovice, Heilbronn, Karlsruhe, Rastatt, Herrenalb, Stuttgart, Regensburg, Linz, Kehl, Tübingen, Danube, Freudenstadt, Horb, Ulm, Munich, Braunau, Freiburg, Biberach, Rosenheim, Salzburg, Berchtesgaden, Basle, Dornbirn, Innsbruck, St. Anton, Vipiteno, Bolzano

Rivers / regions: Ems, Aller, Elba, Oder, Weser, Rhine, Sieg, Fulda, Werra, Thüringerwald, Saale, Mulde, Main, Neckar, Altmühl, Lauter, Inn, Black Forest

Army labels: Can. II Corps, 21st Army Group, Br. XII Corps, Br. XXX Corps, Br. VIII Corps, Can. 1st Army, Br. 2nd Army, U.S. 9th Army, U.S. 15th Army, 12th Army Group, U.S. XVIII Airborne Corps, U.S. VIII Corps, U.S. VII Corps, U.S. XX Corps, U.S. 1st Army, U.S. 3rd Army, U.S. 7th Army, Fr. 1st Army, 6th Army Group, U.S. V Corps, U.S. XII Corps, U.S. III Corps

Legend

- AREA OCCUPIED BY MARCH 27 1945
- AREA OCCUPIED BY APRIL 9
- AREA OCCUPIED BY APRIL 19
- AREA OCCUPIED BY MAY 7
- ALLIED ATTACKS
- GERMAN POCKETS
- ① FIRST RUSSO-BRITISH CONTACT MAY 2
- ② FIRST RUSSO-AMERICAN CONTACT APRIL 25
- ③ CONTACT WITH U.S. 5TH ARMY MAY 4
- RUSSIAN ATTACK APRIL 16
- ·×××× ARMY GROUP BOUNDARIES

CHAPTER 148
The End in Italy

Lt.-Col. Alan Shepperd

△ Sherman tank of the U.S. 1st Armoured Division moves up towards Lucca before the campaign to break the Gothic Line.

iginally known as the Apennine osition, the Gothic Line ran across the ountains, coast to coast, for 200 miles, om near La Spezia on the Gulf of Genoa Pesaro on the Adriatic. It was longer an the line through Cassino, and the ountain barrier reached across the ninsula to within a short distance of ute 16, which followed the coast-line rough the narrow plain to Rimini. ders for the line to be reconnoitred d fortified had in fact been given by dl almost a month before the evacua-on of Sicily, but more recently the work d been interrupted by the pressing mands for *matériel* and labour for ilding the defences of the Gustav d Hitler Lines.

At the time of the capture of Rome, Alexander estimated that Kesselring would have only the equivalent of ten divisions to man the Apennine positions, but Hitler's immediate reaction to the threat of an Allied advance into northern Italy had completely changed the situation. Kesselring was now able to gain much-needed time for the Organisation Todt to complete most of the defences that had been so carefully planned.

At the very height of the fighting in Normandy, Hitler dispatched no less than seven divisions, withdrawn from Denmark, Holland, Hungary, and even the Russian front, to reinforce Army Group "C" in Italy. Finally O.K.W. sent a battalion of Tiger tanks from

▽ German reinforcements en route to the Italian front. The two vehicles in the foreground are ex-Austrian Army "Mulus" wheeled/tracked carriers, and the conventional vehicles appear to be civilian vehicles taken over by the military.

France and the whole of three divisions, forming in Germany, to fill up the ranks of the infantry divisions that had been virtually annihilated in the Liri valley.

Although Alexander had been warned as early as May 22, 1944, that he must be prepared to provide seven divisions for a landing in the south of France, it was not until July 5, when the battle for Arezzo was in the balance and the Polish II Corps was still short of Ancona, that he was told that his pleas to be allowed to keep his force intact, for a thrust into northern Italy and beyond, had finally been turned down.

The task that Alexander was now given was:

1. to cross the Apennines to the line the River Po; and
2. to cross the river and seize the li Venice – Padua – Verona – Bresc

After this he would receive further structions.

In spite of the loss of so many divisio including the French Expeditiona Corps with all its mountain troops, t Allied offensive must continue. On again Kesselring would have superiori in numbers on the ground and strong fortified positions on which to make l stand. The summer days were runni out and the chance of any large sca penetration into the Po valley befo winter set in now appeared most unlikel But in Normandy the Battle of Caen w bout to start—it was imperative that he pressure by the Allies in Italy should e maintained, even increased.

So long as there had been hopes of a apid advance, the bridges over the o had been spared by the Allied bombers. n July 12 the Tactical Air Force went o work and in three days cut all 23 of the ail and road bridges over the river. The attle for the Gothic Line had begun.

Superb defences

n the mountains the German engineers ad already constructed a series of strongoints astride the routes leading to the o valley at Borgo a Mozzano, Porretta, the Vernio pass north of Prato, and the Futa and Il Giogo passes north of Florence. From here the line ran south-east, again with every route blocked, from Casaglia to below Bagno and the Mandrioli pass, before turning eastwards to drop down to the valley of the Foglia and Pesaro on the Adriatic. Here, in the narrow coastal plain, was Route 16, the only road that the Allies could take which did not entail climb across the great mountain barrier. This corridor, however, between the foothills and the sea, was cut across by numerous rivers; and the succession of ridges, which similarly were at right angles to the line of advance, was admirably suited for defence. Moreover, the rivers were liable to sudden flooding and rain quickly turned the heavy soil into a sea

△ *Lieutenant-Colonel J. Sokol, of the Polish 3rd Carpathian Infantry Division, inspects U.S. artillery positions. The division formed part of the Polish II Corps that took Pesaro.*

▽ *Canadian armour crosses the Sieve, which flows into the Arno at Pontassieve, ten miles east of Florence.*

completed when the battle started liste 2,376 machine gun nests, 479 anti-tan gun, mortar, and assault gun positions 120,000 yards of wire entanglement, an many miles of anti-tank ditches. Onl four out of the 30 7.5-cm Panther gu turrets ordered by O.K.W., howeve were in position.

The balance of forces in the openin stages of the forthcoming battle pitted 2 German divisions, including six Panze and *Panzergrenadier* divisions, and som six Italian divisions, against 20 Allie divisions, which included four armoure divisions. For the Germans the battl would be fought solely on the ground as the Luftwaffe in Italy was reduced t 170 aircraft, the majority of which wer obsolete. The Allies, with some 75 com plete squadrons in the Tactical Ai Force alone, enjoyed complete ai superiority. This advantage, howeve would soon be reduced as the weathe deteriorated. Meanwhile Kesselrin could neither "see over the hill", no strike out at his enemy's rear communica tions. In spite of this and a weakness i both artillery and armour, he viewed hi task of beating off the coming offensiv with growing confidence, especially afte an inspection of the defences o his eastern flank.

Throughout the whole campaign th Germans had overestimated the Allie capability to carry out amphibious oper tions against their rear and Kesselrin sensitive to the preparations fo "Dragoon" (as "Anvil" was now name feared a landing on the Ligurian coa or even in the Gulf of Venic Consequently he allocated no less tha six divisions to coastal defence. A furthe weakening of his forces resulted from th active resistance, backed by the Co munists, of Italian workers in the indu trial areas to Mussolini's puppet gover ment. In effect civil war had broken ou and in spite of the arrival of two Germa trained Italian divisions the partisa were also beginning to show their tr strength in attacks on military depo and lines of communication. Thus the remained only 19 divisions to hold t Gothic Line itself. On the right was t 14th Army, with XIV Panzer Corps alloc ted to the long mountain stretch from t coast to Empoli, and I Parachute Cor to hold the shorter and more critic central section facing Florence, bo with three divisions. In reserve were t inexperienced 20th Luftwaffe Field Di

of mud. The fortifications in this sector had been skilfully prepared, with anti-tank ditches, extensive minefields, and the usual deep bunkers. In June and July, while Kesselring's rearguards were slowly falling back through Lombardy, Todt engineers, with thousands of conscripted Italian labourers, were frantically engaged in constructing a ten mile deep belt of obstacles along the whole line, and in the mountains a series of positions to link up with the main strongholds, so as to form a continuous front. A report on the defences that had been on and the 29th *Panzergrenadier* Division, north of Florence. East of Pon-ssieve was the 10th Army, with LI ountain Corps (five divisions) holding e spine of the Apennine range as far as nsepolcro and LXXVI Panzer Corps the foothills and coastal plain, again th five divisions, of which two were heloned back watching the coast. The wly arrived 98th Division was in army serve around Bologna. This again aphasised Kesselring's preoccupation th the central section of the mountain rrier, which was only 50 miles deep at is point, in spite of his prediction that e attack would be made on the Adriatic nk. Meanwhile the front line remained the line of the Arno.

evised plans

exander's initial plan was to press an rly attack, with both armies side by le, into the mountains on the axis Florence–Bologna. Indeed the cover plan, with fake wireless traffic and soldiers arriving in the Adriatic sector wearing Canadian I Corps flashes, had already started. But this was before Clark's 5th Army was reduced to a single corps and the total strength of both armies to 20 divisions. Moreover there was no chance of any reinforcements other than the U.S. 92nd (Negro) Division in September and a Brazilian division by the end of October. So there could be no diversionary operations and no reserve to maintain the impetus of the advance. In spite of this, General Harding, Alexander's chief-of-staff, recommended the plan should stand. Lieutenant-General Sir Oliver Leese, the 8th Army commander, whose troops would have to bear the brunt of the fighting, felt there was a far better chance of breaking through on the Adriatic sector, where his superiority in tanks and guns could be employed to greater effect.

Furthermore General Clark would have greater freedom to make his own dis-

△ *German infantry move down through the Dolomites from Austria towards the front.*
▽ *American motor transport in typical Italian terrain. The problems faced by the attackers in such country were particularly difficult: firstly the logistic difficulties of moving up men and supplies, and then the tactical disadvantage of having to attack uphill.*

▷ *An anti-tank mine clearing platoon of the U.S. 85th Division prepares to clear the approaches to a Bailey bridge being built by the 255th Combat Engineers of the U.S. IV Corps across a gorge on Route 64, south of Bologna.*
▽ *Vergato, south of Bologna: an M24 Chaffee of the 81st Reconnaissance Squadron of the U.S. 1st Armoured Division rolls confidently into the ruins.*
△▷ *U.S. infantry south of Bologna.*
▽▷ *American forces in the Piazza del Campo in Siena.*

sitions. This plan suited one of Alexan-
r's favourite strategies, the "two-han-
d punch", in that by striking at both
venna and Bologna the enemy's re-
rves would be split. At a secret meeting
Orvieto airfield on August 4 between
e two commanders, with only Harding
esent, the matter was decided by
exander in favour of Leese's alter-
tive proposal. As practically the whole
the 8th Army had to be moved across
e mountains to the east coast, D-day
s put back to August 25. The cover
an was put into reverse, with 5th Army
ing told to make "ostentatious pre-
rations" for an attack against the
ntre of the mountain positions. In the
eatest secrecy the regrouping of both
mies was started immediately.

The transfer to north of Ancona of the
lk of the 8th Army—two complete
rps headquarters, some eight divi-
ons, and a mass of corps troops, with
er 80,000 vehicles—was achieved in
days. This was a remarkable feat as
ere were only two roads over the moun-
ins, and both had been systematically
molished by the Germans during their
treat. In many places the roads had to
entirely rebuilt and no less than 40
iley bridges were constructed by the
yal Engineers before the roads could
reopened. Even so the roads were
rgely one-way, and the movement tables
re further complicated by the need to
erate the tank transporters on a con-
nuous shuttle service as a result of the
ort time available for the concen-
ation of the tank brigades.

Meanwhile the British XIII Corps, of
ree divisions under Lieutenant-General
dney Kirkman, joined the U.S. 5th
my, so as to be ready alongside U.S. II
rps to deliver the second blow of "the
o-handed punch" towards Bologna.
e remaining two U.S. divisions, joined
the 6th South African Armoured
vision and a mixed force of American
d British anti-aircraft and other sup-
rt units, hastily trained as infantry,
rmed Major-General Crittenberger's
S. IV Corps. This had the task of holding
e remainder of the 5th Army front. On
e inner flank, acting as a link between
e two armies, was X Corps, with the
th Indian Division, a tank brigade, and
veral "dismounted" armoured car regi-
ents. Every other available man of the
h Army was committed to the main
sault on the right flank.

Leese's plan was to break into the

Gothic Line defences on a narrow front,
with the Polish II Corps directed on
Pesaro (before going into reserve), and
the Canadians making straight for
Rimini. The main attack would be through
the hills further inland towards Route 9
by Lieutenant-General Sir Charles
Keightley's V Corps, with the British 4th,
46th, and 56th, and 1st Armoured Divisions, and 4th Indian Division. The
latter was briefed for the pursuit, and
would attack alongside the Canadian
5th Armoured Division as soon as the
breakthrough was achieved.

The offensive falters

Initially all went well. When the Allied
advance started the Germans were engaged in carrying out a series of reliefs in
the coastal area, which involved the
pulling back of a division from forward
positions on the Metauro. Kesselring
indeed assumed that the attack on August
25 was no more than a follow-up of this
withdrawal. Vietinghoff himself was on
leave and only got back late on August
28. The next day the Allied infantry
reached the Foglia and Kesselring, who
had been taken completely by surprise,
at last ordered up reinforcements. But it
was too late to stop the penetration of the
carefully prepared Gothic Line positions. On August 31 the 46th Division
held the formidable bastion of Montegridolfo and the following night Gurkhas
of the 4th Indian Division, using only
grenades and kukris, captured the strongly fortified town of Tavoleto. In the plain,

the Canadians had suffered heavily cro
ing the river but by dawn on Septemb
3 had a bridgehead across the Con
alongside Route 16. Meanwhile both t
26th Panzer and 98th Divisions h
reached the battle area and alrea
suffered heavily.

The way to a breakthrough by V Cor
lay in the capture of two hill features, t
Coriano and Gemmano Ridges, situat
just where the plain begins to widen ou
These afforded the Germans excelle
observation and fine positions. The ta
of breaking through was given to t
46th and 56th Divisions. Meanwhile, t
British 1st Armoured Division, with so
300 tanks, had already started (on Augu
31) to move forward in accordance wi
the original plan. The approach mar
over narrow and often precipitous trac
which got progressively worse, proved
nightmare. On one stage "along razo
edged mountain ridges" to reach t
Foglia, which was crossed on Septemb
3, drivers of the heavier vehicles had
reverse to get round every corner a
some spent 50 hours at the wheel. T
tank route proved even more hazardo
and 20 tanks were lost before reachi
the assembly area. The driving co
ditions were extremely exhausting a
as the column ground its way forwa
in low gear many tanks ran out of petr
while those at the rear of the column we
engulfed in dense clouds of choking whi
dust.

At this critical moment the Germ
162nd Division and Kesselring's la
mobile reserve, the experienced 29
Panzergrenadier Division (from Bolo
na) began to arrive. The renewed attac

The American M24 Chaffee light tank

Weight: 18 tons.
Crew: 5.
Armament: one 75-mm M6 gun with 48 rounds, and one .5-inch Browning M2 and two .3-inch Browning M1919A4 machine guns with 420 and 4,125 rounds respectively.
Armour: hull front and sides 25-mm, lower sides and rear 19-mm, decking 13-mm, and belly 6.5-mm; turret front and mantlet 38-mm, sides 25-mm, and roof 13-mm.
Engines: two Cadillac Model 44T24 inlines, 110-hp each.
Speed: 30 mph.
Range: 100 miles.
Length: 18 feet.
Width: 9 feet 8 inches.
Height: 8 feet 1½ inches.

▽ 155-mm M1 howitzers of the U.S. 85th Division are towed across the Reno at Pioppi di Salvaro by tracked prime movers.

▷ British infantry rest by a roadside during the closing stages of the Italian campaign. Note the tank destroyers on the road and the weapons carried by the infantry platoon: Lee Enfield rifles, Bren guns, a P.I.A.T. anti-tank weapon, and American M3 sub-machine guns.

▽▷ British infantry bring in two German wounded abandoned by their comrades along the Metauro river.

by V Corps were broken up and held. Into the confused and unresolved struggle the armoured divisions were ordered forward late on September 4. There had been no breakthrough; the fleeting opportunity, if it had ever existed, had passed. The advance of the armoured brigades was met with a storm of shot and shell and an unbroken defence which now included tanks and self-propelled guns. In their advance towards Coriano, the British armoured brigades lost 65 tanks and many more were still struggling to cross the start line as dusk came.

That night rain began to fall and more German reinforcements (from the 356th Division) reached the front. By September 6 the tracks had turned to mud and air

strikes could no longer be guarante Alexander now ordered a regroupi for a set-piece attack (on September to clear the two vital ridges. Now w the time for Clark to launch his atta into the mountains.

Since early August Kesselring's fre line troops had been kept short of suppl through the interdiction programme the Allied air forces. With the Bren pass frequently blocked, north Italy v virtually isolated from the rest of Euro There was no direct railway traffic acr the Po east of Piacenza and south of t river the railway lines down as far the Arno had been cut in nearly 100 plac But in spite of every difficulty, suffici supplies were kept moving forward. Ea

ght, pontoon bridges were built across
e Po and then broken up and hidden
 day; and ferries were operating at
er 50 points on the river.
The Desert Air Force, which had sup-
rted the 8th Army so magnificently at
time when almost all the American
 effort had been diverted to the "Dra-
on" landing, now switched its whole
ort to helping Clark's offensive to get
der way. Clark's attack came as no
rprise to General Joachim Lemelsen,
ose 14th Army had already been milked
 three divisions to reinforce Colonel-
neral Heinrich von Vietinghoff's
th Army. The latter was now seriously
ort of infantry, and had been ordered
 fall back to the prepared defences in

The Italian FIAT G.55 *"Centauro"* fighter

Engine: one FIAT R.A.1050 R.C.58 *Tifone* inline, 1,475-hp
Armament: one 20-mm Mauser MG 151 cannon with 250 rounds, two MG 151 cannon with 200 rounds per gun, and two 12.7-mm Breda-SAFAT machine guns with 300 rounds per gun.
Speed: 385 mph at 22,965 feet.
Climb: 7 minutes 12 seconds to 19,685 feet.
Ceiling: 42,650 feet.
Range: 746 miles.
Weight empty/loaded: 5,952/8,179 lbs.
Span: 38 feet 10½ inches.
Length: 30 feet 8⅞ inches.
Height: 10 feet 3¼ inches.
(This is an aircraft serving with the air force of the Italian Socialist Republic.)

Local intelligence for an American soldier.

he mountains. Even after the transfer o his command of the 334th Division from he adjacent LI Mountain Corps, Lemel-en had no reserve and with all his force n the line, each division was on at least a en mile front. From his post on the "touch-line", as it were, in the quiet and naccessible Ligurian coastal sector, General von Senger und Etterlin orrectly forecast the outcome of this mpasse. He later wrote:

"The incessant prodding against [the eft wing of] our front across the Futa ass was like jabbing a thick cloth with sharp spear. The cloth would give way ike elastic, but under excessive strain it vould be penetrated by the spear."

The 5th Army attack was made by two orps and on a narrow front east of the l Giogo pass, at the junction of the two German armies, and initially fell on two hinly stretched divisions. Holding the l Giogo pass was the 4th Parachute Division, which had been made up with very young soldiers with barely three months' training. The pass itself was nothing but a way over a ridge only about 2,900 feet high, but overlooked by some of the highest peaks in the whole moun-tain range.

Clark used Lieutenant-General Geoffrey Keyes's II Corps of four divi-sions (U.S. 34th, 85th, 88th, and 91st) as his spearhead against the Il Giogo defences. On the tail of the German withdrawal he launched his offensive on September 13. Once again, Kesselring misread the situation. In spite of the efforts of two U.S. divisions, a consider-able artillery concentration, and 2,000 sorties by medium and fighter-bombers, the 4th Parachute Division more than held its ground for the first four days. Meanwhile Kirkman's XIII Corps was attacking on the right flank of the Ameri-cans along the parallel routes towards Faenza and Forlì. By September 14 the 8th Indian Division was over the water-shed and the following day the British 1st Division took Monte Prefetto and, turning to help its neighbours, attacked the German parachute troops on Monte Pratone. As the pressure mounted on the 4th Parachute Division, the leading American infantry began to make ground, and between September 16 and 18 Monti Altuzzo and Monticelli and the nearby strongholds and peaks were captured.

△ *A British officer surveys the final goal of the Italian campaign: the Alps and Austria.*
▷ *Medical corpsmen of the U.S. 10th Mountain Division treat a wounded German prisoner.*

II Corps now held a seven-mile stretch of the Gothic Line defences either side of the Il Giogo pass. At last Kesselring awoke to the danger of a breakthrough to Imola and from either flank rushed in an extra division to hold Firenzuola and the road down the Santerno valley. This was indeed a critical sector for the Germans, for it was one of the few areas on the northern slopes of the mountains where any quantity of artillery and transport could be deployed once over the watershed.

By September 27 Clark's infantry had fought its way forward to within ten miles of Route 9 at Imola, before being halted by fierce and co-ordinated counter-attacks by no less than four German divisions. In attempting to recapture Monte Battaglia, Kesselring threw in units from many divisions, including some pulled out from the Adriatic front, against the U.S. 88th Division. The battle lasted for over a week before the exhausted German infantry was ordered to dig in. But with mounting casualties and deteriorating weather, Clark also

called a halt and turned his attention t[o] Route 65, which would lead him t[o] Bologna.

Coriano ridge taken

On the 8th Army front the Canadians an[d] V Corps resumed the offensive on th[e] night of September 12 and drove th[e] Germans off the Coriano and Gemman[o] ridges, but it took the Canadians thre[e] whole days of bitter and costly fightin[g] to clear San Fortunato. On Septembe[r] 20, Rimini fell to the 3rd Greek Mountai[n] Brigade, who fought well in this its firs[t] engagement, and the following day Allie[d] patrols were across the Marecchia. No[w] as Freyberg's 2nd New Zealand Div[i-] sion passed through on Route 16, th[e] rivers were filling and near spate and th[e] heavy soil of the Romagna was beginnin[g] to grip both men and vehicles as the[y] struggled forward. The Romagna is a[n] immense flat expanse of alluvial so[il] carried down by a dozen or so rivers an[d]

numerable smaller watercourses that
scharge into the Adriatic. Reclaimed
d cultivated over centuries, it is still
sentially a swamp, criss-crossed by
tches and with the watercourses chan-
lled between floodbanks that rise in
aces 40 feet above the plain. Moreover,
e numerous stone-built farmhouses and
mlets, vineyards, and long rows of
uit trees afforded the defence ready-
ade strongpoints and cover. In-
spicious terrain indeed, with all the
ds against a rapid advance. By the 29th
ly the leading elements of the New
aland and 56th Divisions had reached
e banks of the River Fiumicino and the
rmans were still entrenched in the foot-
lls south of Route 9. Torrential rain,
wever, brought all forward movement
a halt, sweeping away bridges and
king fords impassable. But in the
untains X Corps still fought on and
October 8 was within ten miles of
sena.

General Leese, who had been given
mmand of the Allied Land Forces in
uth-East Asia, had now been succeeded
General Sir Richard McCreery. The
w army commander, deciding to avoid
e low ground, launched in succession
e 10th Indian Division and the Poles
rough the mountains. And by October
Cesena had been taken and bridge-
ads seized over the Savio. After resist-
g for four days the Germans voluntarily
thdrew to the line of the Ronco.

Striking now towards Bologna, Clark's
Corps met growing resistance. Initially
had benefited from heavy air support,
cluding strategic bombers, and the
orts of the 8th Army to break out along
ute 9. It had been opposed by less than
o divisions. By the time it reached the
vergano escarpment, however, it was
ed by no less than five divisions (in-
ding the 16th S.S. Panzer Division),
d elements from three other divisions.
is was the work of von Senger, who was
nporarily in command of the 10th
my owing to the illness of Lemelsen.
lped by a spell of fine weather, which
ve the Allied air forces the chance to
ervene, II Corps drove the Germans
the escarpment on October 14. But
n Senger was bringing in more and
re troops and had the defences of
logna properly co-ordinated and well
vered by artillery. Although the 88th
vision captured Monte Grande on
tober 20, with the assistance of fighter-
mbers and the expenditure of 8,600

△ *American troops in Monghidoro.*

▽ *Bailey bridge at Vergato, named after the late president of the United States.*

rounds of gun ammunition, the Americans were beaten back from the little village of Vedriano on three successive nights by fierce counter-attacks.

Since September 10, in just over six weeks II Corps had lost 15,716 men, and over 5,000 of these casualties had been in the 88th Division. On October 25, Clark gave the order to dig in. He himself chose to share some of the discomforts of his men and proposed to sit the winter out in his caravan near the Futa pass, one of the highest parts of the Apennines.

On the other flank, the 8th Army's operations were similarly halted; the weather had broken completely and both sides were exhausted. Alexander wrote that "the rain, which was at that time spoiling Fifth Army's attack on Bologna, now reached a high pitch of intensity. On 26th October all bridges over the Savio, in our immediate rear, were swept away and our small bridge heads over the Ronco were eliminated and destroyed."

Since August the Germans had lost 8,000 prisoners, and LXXVII Panzer Corps alone had suffered over 14,500 battle casualties. Over a third of Kesselring's 92 infantry battalions were down to 200 men each and only ten mustered ov 400. In the 8th Army, battle casualti since July totalled 19,975, and eve infantry battalion had to be reorganise Tank casualties were well over 400 a the 1st Armoured Division had to disbanded.

Winter war

In north-west Europe all chances of decisive victory over Nazi Germany 1944 ended with the reverse at Arnh and the delay in opening the port of A werp. A winter campaign was now evitable. In Italy, Kesselring's Operati "*Herbstnebel*" (Autumn Fog), to short his line by withdrawing to the Alps, w peremptorily turned down by Hitl Alexander's long-term proposal for enveloping attack by landing in Yu slavia could make no immediate cont bution to Eisenhower's present predi ment and indeed proved to be a pipe dre that for political reasons alone wou never have been authorised. So it was t mixture as before, with Hitler s obsessed with the Balkans, Kesselri

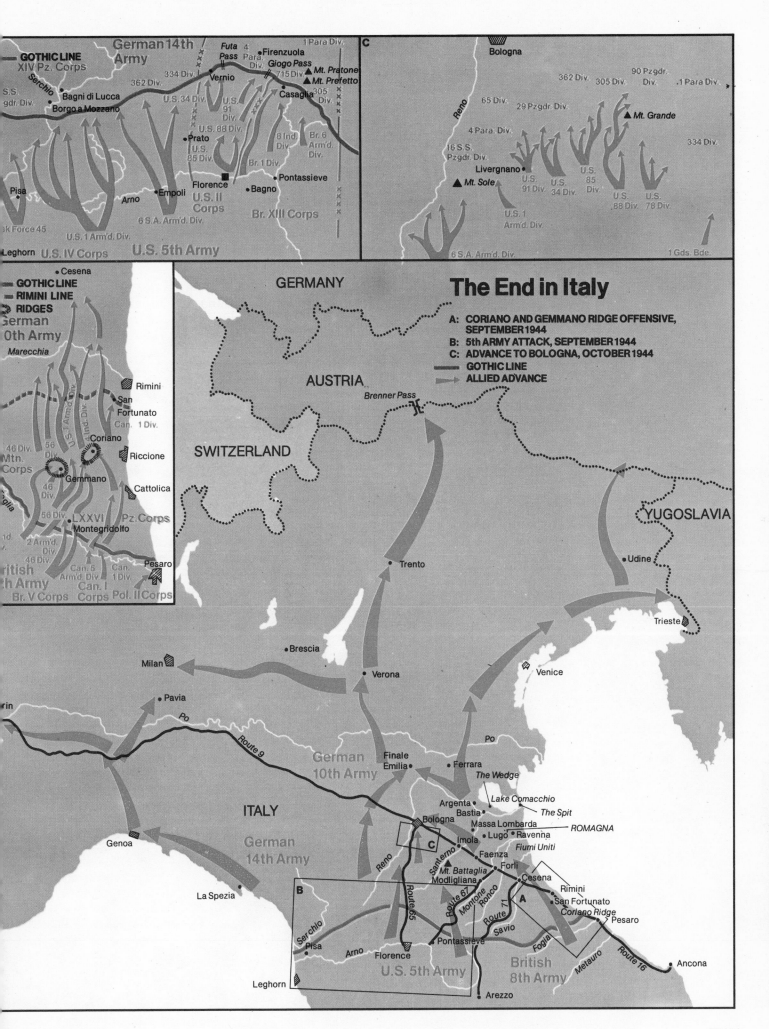

GOTHIC LINE
XIV Pz. Corps

German 14th Army

Futa Pass

Firenzuola

4 Para. Div.

1 Para. Div.

334 Div.

Giogo Pass

Vernio

362 Div.

715 Div.

▲ Mt. Pratone
▲ Mt. Prefetto

S.S. gdr. Div.

Serchio

Bagni di Lucca

Borgo a Mozzano

U.S. 34 Div.

U.S. 91 Div.

Casaglia

305 Div.

U.S. 88 Div.

U.S. 85 Div.

Prato

8 Ind. Div.

Br. 6 Arm'd. Div.

Br. 1 Div.

Pisa

Empoli

Arno

Florence

U.S. II Corps

Bagno

Pontassieve

Br. XIII Corps

k Force 45

6 S.A. Arm'd. Div.

Leghorn

U.S. 1 Arm'd. Div.

U.S. IV Corps

U.S. 5th Army

C

Bologna

362 Div.

305 Div.

90 Pzgdr. Div.

.1 Para. Div.

Reno

65 Div.

29 Pzgdr. Div.

4 Para. Div.

▲ Mt. Grande

334 Div.

16 S.S. Pzgdr. Div.

Livergnano

U.S. 85 Div.

▲ Mt. Sole

U.S. 91 Div.

U.S. 34 Div.

U.S. 88 Div.

U.S. 78 Div.

U.S. 1 Arm'd. Div.

6 S.A. Arm'd. Div.

1 Gds. Bde.

Cesena

GOTHIC LINE
RIMINI LINE
RIDGES

German 0th Army

Marecchia

Rimini

San Fortunato

Can. 1 Div.

U.S. 1 Arm'd. Div.

Coriano

46 Div.

56 Div.

Riccione

Mtn. Corps

46 Div.

Gemmano

Cattolica

56 Div.

LXXVI Pz. Corps

Montegridolfo

2 Arm'd. Div.

46 Div.

ritish th Army

Can. 5 Arm'd. Div.

Can. 1 Div.

Can. I Corps

Pesaro

Br. V Corps

Pol. II Corps

The End in Italy

A: CORIANO AND GEMMANO RIDGE OFFENSIVE, SEPTEMBER 1944
B: 5th ARMY ATTACK, SEPTEMBER 1944
C: ADVANCE TO BOLOGNA, OCTOBER 1944

━━━ GOTHIC LINE
➤ ALLIED ADVANCE

GERMANY

AUSTRIA

Brenner Pass

SWITZERLAND

YUGOSLAVIA

Udine

Trento

Trieste

Brescia

Venice

Milan

Verona

Pavia

rin

Po

Route 9

Po

Finale Emilia

Ferrara

ITALY

German 10th Army

The Wedge

Argenta

Lake Comacchio

Bastia

The Spit

Massa Lombarda

Genoa

German 14th Army

Reno

Bologna

Imola

Lugo

Ravenna

ROMAGNA

Faenza

Fiumi Uniti

Forlì

La Spezia

Santerno

Mt. Battaglia

Modligliana

Cesena

Rimini

B

Route 65

Route 67

Montone

Ronco

San Fortunato

Serchio

Pisa

Arno

Florence

Pontassieve

Savio

Fogia

Coriano Ridge

Pesaro

A

Route 71

Leghorn

U.S. 5th Army

Arezzo

Metauro

Route 16

Ancona

British 8th Army

2341

over-sensitive of his coastal flank on t
Adriatic, but ordered to fight where
stood, and Alexander with dwindli
resources committed to a continuati
of the battle of attrition against the gra
of the country and in the most adver
climatic conditions. Furthermore, t
bad weather was seriously limiting t
use of Allied air power, at a time wh
the Allies were facing a world-wi
shortage of certain types of artille
ammunition as a result of the extr
ordinarily sanguine and premature c
cision to set back production.

The fighting continued until ear
January, with the Allies aiming to rea
Ravenna and break the line of the Sa
terno before reviewing the thrust
Bologna. In the north "Ponterforce

sisting of Canadian and British ar-
ured units and named after its com-
nder, co-operating with "Popski's Pri-
e Army" of desert fame, reached the
ks of the Fiumi Uniti and Ravenna
lf fell to I Canadian Corps. Soon the
nadians reached the southern tip of
ke Comacchio, but it was only after a
rce and costly battle that they were
e to force the Germans back behind
line of the Senio. Astride Route 9,
acking westwards, V Corps captured
nza, and in the foothills south of the
d the Poles fought forward to the
er reaches of the Senio. At this point
5th Army was stood-to at 48 hours'
ice on December 22 to resume the
ack.

ut the weather again broke and by a
rk of fate Mussolini, despised by
nd and foe alike, and seeking a "spec-
ular" success for his newly formed
isions, made a last throw in a losing
ne. These two divisions, the "Monte
sa" and the "Italia" Bersaglieri Divi-
ns, led by the German 148th Division,
v launched a counter-attack on the
reme left flank of the 5th Army. This
ance towards the vital port of Leg-
n came on the very day that virtually
whole of the 5th Army was concen-
ted and poised ready to attack
ogna. Only the 92nd (Negro) Division,
ted around Bagni di Lucca, was in
ition to meet the attack down the
d and romantic valley of the Serchio.
arrival of 8th Indian Division on
cember 25 was only just in time to stop
omplete breakthrough, as the leading
rman units overran the two main
ence lines before being held and driven
k by the Indians. Meanwhile this
eat to the main supply base had caused
more of the 5th Army's divisions to
switched from the main battle area,
with heavy snow falling in the moun-
is, Alexander gave the order for both
ies to pass to the defensive.

mmand shuffles

ring the winter months there were
nges in command on both sides. On
death of Sir John Dill, head of the
tish mission to Washington, Maitland
son was sent in his place and Alexan-
became Supreme Allied Commander
diterranean, with promotion to
ld-Marshal, backdated to the capture

of Rome. Clark now commanded the
15th Army Group, and Truscott was
recalled from France to take over the
5th Army. On the German side Lemelsen
still commanded the 14th Army and
General Traugott Herr, whose corps had
held the early attacks on the Adriatic
flank, the 10th Army in what was to prove
the critical eastern sector. Kesselring
left in the middle of March to become
O.B. West and Vietinghoff, hurriedly
recalled from the Baltic, took his place
with unequivocal orders from Hitler to
hold every yard of ground. This further
example of the Führer's inept "rigid
defence" doctrine proved disastrous, as
Vietinghoff entered the ring for the final
round of the campaign like a boxer with
his bootlaces tied together!

In conditions of heavy snow and frost,
the struggle on both sides was now against
the forces of nature, and the Allied supply
routes could only be kept open by the daily
and unremitting efforts of thousands of
civilians and all but those units in the
most forward positions. While the Germans hoarded their meagre supplies of
petrol and both sides built up stocks of
ammunition, the Allied units at last
began to receive some of the specialised
equipment they had for so long been
denied; "Kangaroos", the Sherman tanks
converted to carry infantry; D.D.s, the
amphibious tanks that had swum ashore
onto the Normandy beaches; and "Fantails", tracked landing vehicles for shal-
low waters, of which 400 were promised
for use on Lake Comacchio and the nearby flooded areas. At the same time the
armoured regiments were re-equipped
with up-gunned Sherman and Churchill
tanks, Tank-dozers, and "Crocodile"
flame-throwing tanks, many of which
were fitted with "Platypus" tracks to
compete with the soft ground of the
Romagna. Throughout the remaining
winter months the "teeth" arms were
busy training with new assault equipment, such as bridge-laying tanks and
flame throwers. The experience of the
British 78th Division, back after refitting
in the Middle East, is a typical example
of the hard work put into preparing for
the spring offensive.

"Training began almost at once—
exercises for testing communications, in
river crossings, in street fighting and,
above all in co-operation with armour.
2 Armoured Brigade . . . was affiliated to
the Division for these exercises . . . it
was the first time in Italy that 78 Division

△ ◁ *In the British V Corps' rear
area: men of the 8th Army get a
chance to have a closer (and
safer!) look at the armoured
vehicles used by the Germans.
Note the hoarding for the
exhibition, featuring Jon's
immortal "Two Types".*
▽ ◁ *British Churchill tanks in
action in the artillery support
rôle.*
△ *German prisoners in Italy.*

S.S. Obergruppenführer *Karl Wolff, military governor of northern Italy and Germany's liaison man with Mussolini. Realising that the war was lost, he negotiated an armistice with the Allies, effective from May 2, 1945.*

▷ *American liberation forces enter the city of Milan, led by an armoured car of the Italian Communist partisans.*

▽ *Knocked-out motor transport in Italy.*

had lived, trained, and held the line with the armour with which it was later to carry out full-scale operations: this was the genesis of the splendid team work between tanks and infantry soon to be shown in the final battle."

Before handing over, Kesselring kept his troops hard at work building defences on every river-line right back to the Reno and indeed on the line of the Po itself. Although milked of forces for the other fronts, his two armies still contained some of the very best German divisions. These were now well up to strength and fully rested, as for instance the two divisions of I Parachute Corps, commanded by the redoubtable General Richard Heidrich, which between them mustered 30,000 men. The active front, however, much of which was on difficult ground not of his own choosing, was 130 miles long, and his supply lines were constantly being attacked from the air and by partisans. To cover his front he

allocated 19 German divisions (includ the 26th Panzer, and 29th and 90th *P zergrenadier*). Five more German fantry divisions, plus four Italian d sions and a Cossack division, were h back to watch the frontiers and, in ticular, to guard against a landing the Gulf of Venice. Here, had he known, sand-bars precluded large-sc amphibious operations.

The relative strength of the 15th A Group was now lower than ever bef Three divisions had been rushed intervene in the civil war in Greece a Canadian Corps had left for Hollan February. There remained only 17 d sions, including the newly arrived Am can 10th Mountain Division. But Alex der held an ace–overwhelming stren in the air. With the combined bom offensive drawing to a close, more more heavy bomber squadrons were leased to support the coming offens and by April were pounding away at

2344

man supply routes. By D-day every
lway line north of the Po had been
in many places. Nor had the two
tical air forces been idle. On February
364 sorties were flown against the
nner pass and targets in the Venetian
in, while in March the German supply
mps, so carefully built-up during the
ter, were systematically attacked.
ove the battlefield, in clearing skies,
Allies' planes roamed at will and
en the offensive opened, a total of
0 aircraft was available to intervene
ectly in the land battle.

e last lap

xander's plan was again for a double-
ed attack, but with a bold and care-
ly set-up change of direction by the
Army at the very moment when the
Army was to deliver the second blow.
ce again the Germans were to be mis-
into expecting a major landing (south
Venice) and realism was brought to
s cover plan by the joint Commando/
h Division operations to clear the
it" and "wedge", on the near shore,
l the islands of Lake Comacchio, which
fact were vital to the real flanking
ust inland. Meanwhile the whole of
8th Army, except for a skeleton force
the mountains, was secretly concen-
ted to the north of Route 9. On 9 April,
Corps (8th Indian and 2nd New Zealand
risions) and the Polish II Corps would
en the offensive across the River Senio
ride Lugo, with the object of seizing
dgeheads over the Santerno and ex-
iting beyond. At this point the 5th
my would attack towards Bologna,
ile the 56th Division would cross Lake
macchio in "Fantails" and the 78th
vision would debouch from the San-
no bridgeheads and strike north-
rds to Bastia. This change of axis by
8th Army aimed at breaking the
nge" of the whole German position
Argenta and cutting their lines of
hdrawal eastwards.
Shortly after mid-day on April 9, the
ied air forces went to work with the
dium bombers and close support squad-
s attacking command posts, gun posi-
ns, and strongpoints on the Senio and
rond, while in an hour and a half the
avy bombers, using a line of smoke
lls in the sky as a bomb line, saturated
German defences on the immediate

The end of the road for Hitler's armies in Italy.
△ *Prisoners taken by the U.S. IV Corps await transfer to a prisoner-of-war camp and, in the long run, repatriation to Germany.*
▷ *British troops with prisoners.*

front of the two assault corps with 125,000 fragmentation bombs. This deluge of bombs was immediately followed by four hours of concentrated gun and mortar fire, alternating with low-level fighter-bomber attacks. At 1900 hours as the last shells burst on the forward defences, the fighter-bombers swept over in a dummy attack to keep the enemy's heads down until the infantry crossed the river. Within minutes the first flame-throwers were in action and "the whole front seemed to burst into lanes of fire". Overnight there was bitter fighting before the western flood banks were breached and bridges laid for the armour and anti-tank guns to cross. The next day over 1,600 Allied heavy bombers renewed their attack, and on the third day of the offensive the New Zealanders were across the Santerno at Massa Lombarda. The German 98th and 362nd Divisions had lost

over 2,000 prisoners and their forwa battalions had been virtually destroye

Meanwhile the battle for the Argen Gap had started. The 78th Divisio having crossed the Santerno, was a vancing rapidly, led by a special strikir force (the Irish Brigade and 2nd Armour Brigade) of all arms, part of which w entirely mounted on tracked vehicl and which became known as the "Ka garoo Army". The approaches to Basti however, were covered by thousands mines and the Germans fought to the l round, while in crossing Lake Comacchi the 58th Division suffered heavy casu ties. But slowly the pincer attacks clos on Argenta itself and McCreery's reser divisions began to move up.

Now was the time for Truscott to laun his two corps, but poor flying conditio delayed the attack until April 14. Ov the next four days the Allied air forc

2346

2347

▷ *Lieutenant-General Frido von Senger und Etterlin discusses the terms for the surrender of the German forces in Italy with Major-General Gruenther in Caserta.*
▽ *The scene outside Milan Cathedral after the liberation of the city.*

flew over 4,000 sorties in support and the first 30 minutes of the attack on Mon Sole and the nearby Monte Rumic 75,000 shells fell on the German mounta strongpoints. In three days' fighting tl U.S. II Corps was held down and advance less than two miles. West of Route 6 however, the 10th Mountain Divisic captured Montepastore and for two da the U.S. 1st Armoured Division and tl 90th *Panzergrenadier* Division, Vietin hoff's last reserve, fought it out in tl valley of the Samoggia. Suddenly tl end was within sight. Around Argen the 29th *Panzergrenadier* Division ar the remnants of a number of other div sions kept up a bitter struggle to preve a breakthrough by the 6th Armour Division, but by April 20 V Corps' leadin columns were within 15 miles of Ferrar advancing on a broad front. Along Rou 9 the New Zealanders and Poles h; fought three German divisions to a stan still and at dawn on April 21 a Poli brigade entered Bologna unopposed. Tl previous day a company of the U.S. 86 Mountain Infantry was across Route west of the city, and now Truscott's Corps, with the 6th South African A moured Division, swept past on Route (On April 23 the leading tanks ma contact with a squadron of 16th/5 Lancers, 15 miles west of Ferrara.

On April 20, Vietinghoff, in defian of Hitler's demands, ordered a wit drawal to the Po, but the fate of his armi was already sealed. What was left of l shattered units was trapped against t Po, where every bridge was down blocked by packed columns of burni vehicles. Von Senger was amongst tho who succeeded in crossing. "At dawn the 23rd we found a ferry at Bergantin of the thirty-six Po ferries in the zone Fourteenth Army, only four were st serviceable. Because of the incessa fighter-bomber attacks it was useless cross in daylight."

When the Allied armoured colum crossed 36 hours later, they left behi them "a scene of extraordinary desol tion and fearful carnage. There was longer any coherent resistance, and alor the river lay the ruins of a German army In the first 14 days of the offensive t German casualties were around 67,00 of whom 35,000 had been taken prison Allied casualties were a little over 16,50 On May 2 the remaining German a Italian troops of Army Group "C", near a million men, surrendered.

The American Douglas A-20G Havoc attack bomber

Engines: two Wright R-2600-23
Double Cyclone radials, 1,600-hp each.
Armament: four 20-mm cannon and
five .5-inch Browning machine guns,
plus up to 4,000 lbs of bombs.
Speed: 317 mph at 10,000 feet.
Ceiling: 25,000 feet.
Range: 1,025 miles.
Weight empty/loaded: 17,200/
24,000 lbs.
Span: 61 feet 4 inches.
Length: 48 feet.
Height: 17 feet 7 inches.
Crew: 3.

After his rescue from the Gran Sasso by Otto Skorzeny on September 12, 1943, Mussolini met Hitler. Together the two leaders decided on the establishment of a new Fascist republic in what was left of Italy, and Mussolini's new government met at La Rocca on September 27. The German leader had no intention, however, of letting Mussolini's government actually run the country and refused to answer letters on the subject. The Fascist régime did manage to try some of those responsible for the July 1943 coup that ousted Mussolini. One of those found guilty and executed was Ciano. Opposition to the régime was growing, however, and in the middle of 1944 it was estimated that over 80,000 partisans were operating against the Fascists and Nazis.

With the final Allied victory imminent, Mussolini left for Como, where he was joined by his mistress, Clara Petacci.

◁◁ *Mussolini's last days: the Duce inspects Fascist militia in Milan. There is little of his earlier swagger left in the "Caesar of the new Roman Empire".*

▽ ◁ *Arrested by Italian partisans on April 26, Mussolini and Clara Petacci were shot down without ceremony on the 28th in the small town of Dongo, near Como. The bodies of Mussolini, Petacci, and other Fascist leaders were then taken to Milan and dumped in the Piazza Loretto, where this photograph was taken.*

◁ *The mutilated bodies of Benito Mussolini and Clara Petacci.*

▽ *After lying in the street for several hours, the bodies were hung from the framework of a garage for the edification of the crowd. Mussolini is third from left and Petacci fourth.*

CHAPTER 149

GERMANY: The trap closes

One of General Bradley's tasks was to reduce the "fortified area of the Ruhr" where, on Hitler's orders, Field-Marshal Model had shut himself in. Given the job of carrying out the operation, the American 15th Army attacked southwards across the Ruhr and westwards across the Sieg.

By April 12, Lieutenant-General Gerow had occupied the entire coal basin in which, despite the *Führerbefehl* of March the Germans had done nothing to add to the destruction wrought by British and American bombing. Two days later, the pocket had been cut in two from north to south. In these conditions, Colonel-

General Harpe, commanding the 5th *Panzerarmee,* recognising the fact that his chief had disappeared, ordered Army Group "B" to cease fighting. Capitulation delivered 325,000 prisoners (including 29 generals) into Allied hands. A vain search was instituted for Field-Marshal Hans Model, and it was learnt only four months later that he had committed suicide on April 21, lest he be handed over to the Russians after his surrender, and had been buried in a forest near Wuppertal.

Without waiting for the outcome here, the American 9th, 1st, and 3rd Armies exploited their advance to the full. Resis-

▽ *American infantry press on into Germany past an enormous concrete air raid shelter in Aix-la-Chapelle. Parked in the lee of the building is a Sherman tank.*

tance grew weaker every day, and the average daily haul of prisoners rose from 10,600 between February 22 and March 31 to 29,000 for the week April 2 to 9, and reached 50,000 in the middle of the month. Evidently, the *Landser* (German "Tommy") was at the end of his tether, in spite of the growing wave of drumhead courts martial and summary executions. In the heart of the Reich, the multiplication of divisions went on almost to the final day, but whether they belonged to the Wehrmacht or to the *Waffen*-S.S., these new divisions, *Panzergrenadier* for the most part, revealed the paucity of their training as soon as they came under fire.

The *Volkssturm*, which was intended to fill the gaps in defence, was a pitiful ragbag of middle-aged men and adolescents, armed and equipped with any weapon that came to hand. Witness the battalion leader, taken prisoner by the Canadian Army, who confided to Major

Shulman:

"'I had 400 men in my battalion,' said, 'and we were ordered to go i the line in our civilian clothes. I told local Party Leader that I could not acc the responsibility of leading men i battle without uniforms. Just bef commitment the unit was given Danish rifles, but there was no ammu tion. We also had four machine-gu and 100 anti-tank bazookas (Panzerfau None of the men had received any tra ing in firing a machine-gun, and they w all afraid of handling the anti-ta weapon. Although my men were qu ready to help their country, they refus to go into battle without uniforms a without training. What can a Volksstu man do with a rifle without ammuniti The men went home. That was the o thing they could do.'"

In these conditions, allowing for spo dic but short-lived retaliation here a

▽ *An American 9th Army infantryman shelters behind a blasted tree as a road mine is exploded. Note the Sherman flail tank on the right, waiting to go into action. The sloping box at its rear contains chalk dust to mark the path cleared.*
▷ *American soldiers examine a Messerschmitt Me 262 fighter-bomber found in the outskirts of a wood. Note the 20-mm cannon shells in the foreground.*
▽▷ *Two soldiers with their families surrender to the British.*

The American Republic P-47M Thunderbolt fighter

227386

Engine: one Pratt & Whitney R-2800-57 radial, 2,800-hp.
Armament: eight .5-inch Browning machine guns with 425 rounds per gun.
Speed: 470 mph at 30,000 feet.
Climb: 3,500 feet per minute at 5,000 feet.
Ceiling: 44,000 feet.
Range: 560 miles without drop tank
Weight empty/loaded: 10,423/ 15,500 lbs.
Span: 40 feet 9⅜ inches.
Length: 36 feet 4 inches.
Height: 14 feet 7 inches

ere from a few units that still retained
ne semblance of order and strength,
e advance of the 12th Army Group
ross Germany gathered speed and took
more and more the character of a
ute march, facilitated by the *Auto-
hn* system, which in by-passing the
wns removed inevitable bottlenecks.
a result, American losses dropped to
ignificant figures. In the 3rd Army,
cording to Patton's record, for three
rps of 12, then 14, divisions, between
arch 22 and May 8, 1945, they amounted
2,160 killed, 8,143 wounded, and 644
ssing, under 11,000 in all, compared
th nearly 15,000 evacuated because of
kness and accidental injury.

On the left of the 12th Army Group, the
merican 9th Army, straddling the *Auto-
hn* from Cologne to Frankfurt-am-
er to the south of Berlin, thrust to-
rds Hannover, which it took on April
and three days later reached Wol-
rstedt on the left bank of the Elbe, 85
les further east. With the capture of
rby, slightly upstream of Magdeburg,
established a first bridgehead on the
ht bank of the river, thus putting its
d Division (Major-General R. C.
con) some 75 miles from the New
ancellery. But then it turned instead
wards Dessau and made contact there
th the 6th Armoured Division (Major-
neral G. W. Read), which was moving
ead of the 1st Army.

The 1st Army had crossed the Weser at
inden and driven across Thuringia
a line linking Göttingen, Nordhausen,
d Eisleben, covering nearly 80 miles
ween April 8 and 12. As has been
ntioned above, it was its left flank that
de contact with the 9th Army's right.
is pincer movement cut off the retreat
the German 11th Army, which had
yed in the Harz mountains as ordered.
clear a way through for withdrawal,
K.W. sent the *"Clausewitz"* Panzer
vision to the rescue. It attacked at the
ction between the 21st and 12th Army
oups and inflicted some damage on
9th Army. But having got 35 to 40
les from its point of departure, in the
ion of Braunschweig, it too was
veloped and annihilated. The same fate
uck the 11th Army, falling almost to a
n into Allied hands.

n the centre of the 1st Army, VIII
rps, after reaching the Elbe, managed
establish a bridgehead at Wittenberg,
ile to its right, VII Corps took Halle
d Leipzig on April 14. The capture

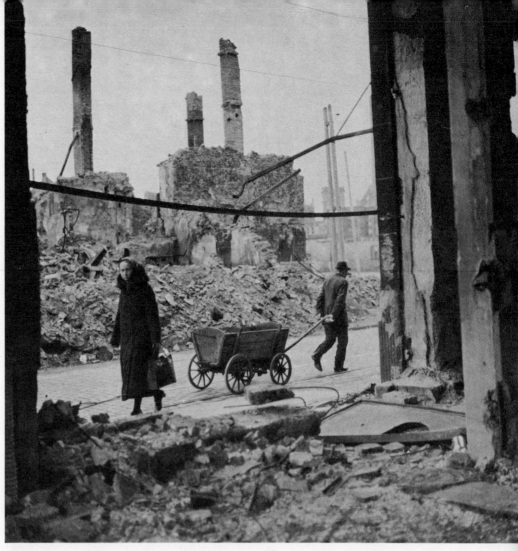

of Leipzig was a combined effort with the
9th Armoured Division, from the 3rd
Army. In accordance with his instructions, General Hodges waited for some
days on the Mulde, and it was only on
April 26 at Torgau that he met up with
Colonel-General Zhadov, commanding
the Soviet 5th Guards Army. In the course
of this rapid advance the 1st Army came
across 300 tons of *Wilhelmstrasse* archives
deposited in various places in the Harz.
At Nordhausen, it occupied the vast
underground factories where most of
the V-1 and V-2 missiles were manufactured.

On March 30 the impetuous Patton was
on the Werra and the Fulda. On April
12, the 3rd Army, changing its direction
from north-east to east, crossed the
Saale at Naumburg, Jena, and Saalfeld,
having broken the last serious resistance
offered by the enemy at Mühlhausen in
Thuringia. And on April 7 the 3rd Army
took the 400,000th prisoner since its
campaign opened. On the 21st following,
XX Corps reached Saxony and the vicinity
of Chemnitz, VIII Corps reached a point
beyond Plauen, while XII Corps, changing
course from east to south-east, had got
well beyond Bayreuth in Bavaria. This
was the last exploit by Manton S. Eddy

△ *Germany* in extremis: *bombed
mercilessly, short of food, and
without motor transport as a
result of the fuel shortage. This
is Darmstadt, which fell to the
26th Division of the U.S. 3rd
Army.*
Overleaf top: *An unfortunate
reminder of better days in
shattered Rheydt–"What have
you done for Germany today?"*
Overleaf bottom: *German
civilians and their protection
against stray bullets.*
Page 2359: *An American motor
transport column, headed by a
jeep, wends its way into Germany.*

who suffered a heart attack and had
hand over his corps to Major-Gener
Stafford LeRoy Irwin. If the 1st Arn
had captured the *Wilhelmstras*
archives, the 3rd discovered the la
reserves of the *Reichsbank,* composed
gold bars worth 500,000,000 francs, sma
quantities of French, Belgian, and Nc
wegian currency and 3,000,000,000 marl
in notes.

An ultimate regrouping by Bradl
switched VIII Corps from Patton's co
mand to Hodges's, and the progressi
collapse of Army Group "B" permitt
III and V Corps to be switched to the 3
Army. Thus strengthened, it was given t
assignment of supporting the activiti
of the 7th Army in Bavaria and upp
Austria; specifically, to prevent the enen
establishing himself in the "nation
redoubt" zone, which General Stron
head of S.H.A.E.F. Intelligence, in
memorandum dated March 11, depict
as follows:

"Here, defended both by nature a
by the most efficient secret weapons y
invented, the powers that have hither
guided Germany will survive to r
organise her resurrection; here arm
ments will be manufactured in bom
proof factories, food and equipment w
be stored in vast underground caver
and a specially selected corps of your
men will be trained in guerrilla wa
fare, so that a whole underground arn
can be fitted and directed to libera
Germany from the occupying forces

Patton advanced with all speed, and
the day of the surrender he had pushe
his XII Corps to a point ten miles belo
Linz on the Austrian Danube, and h
III Corps, whose command had been take
over by Major-General James A. Va
Fleet, as far as Rosenheim at the fo
of the Bavarian Alps. On May 2, h
13th Armoured Division (Major-Gener
Millikin) crossed the Inn at Brauna
birthplace of Adolf Hitler, who had ju
committed suicide in his bunker in t
Berlin Chancellery.

Patton would have liked to complete h
triumph by maintaining the drive of
(Major-General Clarence R. Huebne
and XII Corps as far as Prague. But
May 6, Eisenhower sent him categoric
instructions via Bradley not to go beyo
the Ceské Budejovice–Plzen–Karlo
Vary line in Czechoslovakia which l
had reached. By this action, the Supren
Allied Commander, who had consult
Marshal Antonov, Stalin's Chief-of-Sta

on the matter, yielded to the objections such an operation raised in the Soviet camp. In any event, the American 3rd Army met the spearhead of the 3rd Ukrainian Front, which had come up the Danube from Vienna, at Linz.

Montgomery drives for Lübeck

Montgomery's main task now was to push through to Lübeck and cut off the German forces occupying Norway and Denmark. He put the more energy and dispatch into the task knowing that its accomplishment would bring supplementary benefits:

"With the Rhine behind us we drove hard for the Baltic. My object was to g there in time to be able to offer a fir front to the Russian endeavours to g up into Denmark, and thus control t. entrance to the Baltic."

For this purpose, he disposed of t. British 2nd Army and the Canadian 1 Army, comprising five corps of 16 di sions (six of them armoured). Befo him in Holland he found the Germ: 25th Army, of which General von Blume tritt had just assumed command, and t. debris of the 1st Parachute Army. Th debilitated force had been put under t. overall command of Field-Marshal Busc who had been placed at the head of Northern Defence Zone, to include t. Netherlands, north-west Germany, De mark, and Norway. Weakness in nu: bers and *matériel* was, however, to son extent offset by the fact that tracts

▽ *Stuttgart Cathedral, heavily damaged but still standing amidst the ruins of the rest of the city on March 31, 1945.*

and the otherwise marshy nature of the ground kept the tanks to the main roads.

Having captured Münster, the key to Westphalia, General Dempsey, commanding the British 2nd Army, pushed forward his XXX Corps in the direction of Bremen, XII Corps towards Hamburg, and VIII Corps towards Lübeck. On the right, VIII Corps (Lieutenant-General Sir Evelyn H. Barker) was momentarily delayed by the "Clausewitz" Panzer Division's counter-attack which, as has been mentioned above, was aimed at the point of contact of the 21st and 12th Army Groups. Nonetheless, VIII Corps reached the Elbe opposite Lauenburg on April 19. Here, Montgomery, anxious to move with all possible speed, requested support from Eisenhower and was given the U.S. XVIII Airborne Corps (8th Division, 5th and 7th Armoured Divisions, and the U.S. 82nd Airborne and British 6th Airborne Divisions). On April 29-30, British and Americans under cover provided by the first R.A.F. jet fighters, Gloster Meteors, forced the Elbe. On May 2, 11th Armoured Division (Major-General Roberts), which was the spearhead of the British VIII Corps, occupied Lübeck and the 6th Airborne Division entered Wismar, 28 miles further east, six hours ahead of Marshal Rokossovsky's leading patrols.

Hamburg and Bremen taken

XII Corps (Lieutenant-General Ritchie) had to sustain one last challenge on April 6 when crossing the Aller, a tributary on the right bank of the Weser. Afterwards, it took advantage of the bridgehead won on the Elbe by VIII Corps and closed in on Hamburg. On

▽ Infantry of the 3rd Algerian Division cross the Lauter during their advance towards southern Germany and Austria.

May 2, Lieutenant-General Wolz surrendered the ruins of the great Hanseatic port. Two days later, the 7th Armoured Division (Major-General Lyne) captured intact a bridge over the Kiel Canal at Eckernförde. Ritchie, who was within 35 miles of the town of Flensburg, where Grand-Admiral Dönitz had recently taken over the responsibilities of head of state, had brilliantly avenged the defeat inflicted on him at Tobruk.

In their drive on Bremen, Sir Brian Horrocks and his XXX Corps were held up by a great deal of destruction, and met with altogether fiercer resistance. Before Lingen, what was left of the 7th Parachute Division carried through a hand-to-hand counter-attack with frenetic *"Heil Hitler"* battle cries.

The 2nd *Kriegsmarine* Division showed the same aggressive spirit in defence, and it needed a pincer movement staged by three divisions to bring about the fall of Bremen on April 26. A few hours before the cease-fire, the Guards Armoured Division occupied Cuxhaven at the mouth of the Elbe.

△ *An historic occasion: General Courtney Hodges, commander of the American 1st Army, greets Colonel-General A. S. Zhadov, commander of the Soviet 5th Guards Army, outside Togau on the Elbe on April 25. The Eastern and Western Allies had at last linked up, and Germany had been cut in two.*
◁ *The Möhne dam as the Americans found it in May 1945, rebuilt since the celebrated "dambuster" raid.*

Canadians in Holland

On April 1, General Crerar, commanding the Canadian 1st Army, recovered his II Corps, reinforced by the British 49th Division, thus bringing his divisions up to six. His mission was twofold: to drive between the Weser and the Zuiderzee with the British XXX Corps in the general direction of Wilhelmshaven and Emden; and to liberate the Dutch provinces still occupied by the enemy. The Canadian II Corps (Lieutenant-General Simonds), which had taken part in the crossing of the Rhine, fulfilled the first of these missions. On April 6, it liberated Zutphen and Almelo, and four days later Groningen and Leeuwarden. In this fine action, it was greatly helped by Dutch resistance while the French 2nd and 3rd Parachute Regiments dropped in the area of Assem and Meppel to open a way for it over the Orange Canal. On German territory, however, General Straube's II Parachute Corps put up a desperate fight, and Crerar had to call on Montgomery for help from the Polish 1st Armoured Division, the Canadian 5th Armoured Division, and the British 3rd Division. With this shot of new blood, the Canadian II Corps accelerated its advance and on May

The German *Flakpanzer* IV *"Wirbelwind"* (Whirlwind) self-propelled A.A.mounting

Weight: 25 tons.
Crew: 5.
Armament: one 2-cm *Flakvierling* 38
four-barrelled A.A. gun with 620 rounds.
Armour: hull front 85-mm, hull sides 30-mm, and
turret 15-mm.
Engine: one Maybach HL 120 TRM inline, 300-hp.
Speed: 25 mph on roads and 10 mph cross-country.
Range: 125 miles on roads and 80 miles cross-country.
Length: 18 feet 9½ inches.
Width: 9 feet 4¾ inches.
Height: 8 feet 9½ inches.

1945, General Maczek's Polish 1st
~~moured Division was within nine miles
~~Wilhelmshaven, and the Canadian 5th
~~moured Division on the outskirts of
~~nden.

The Canadian I Corps (Lieutenant-
~~neral C. Foulkes) took Arnhem by
~~ outflanking movement and three days
~~ter reached the Zuiderzee at Harder-
~~jk. The Germans responded to this
~~tack by opening the sea-dykes, and
~~erar, who was concerned to spare
~~e Dutch countryside the ravages of
~~ooding, agreed to a cease-fire with
~~neral von Blumentritt, stipulating in
~~change that British and American
~~rcraft be given free passage to provide
~~e Dutch population with food and
~~edical supplies. This dual operation
~~st the Canadian 1st Army 367 officers
~~d 5,147 N.C.O.s and other ranks killed,
~~unded, and missing.

ast German high
ommand change

~~hile Field-Marshal Busch had been
~~trusted with the command of a "North-
~~ Defence Zone", Kesselring was called
~~on to lead a "Southern Defence Zone"
~~ich included the German forces fight-
~~ between the Main and the Swiss
~~ntier. So during the final phase of the
~~mpaign he found himself facing General
~~vers, whose 6th Army Group numbered
~~ divisions on March 30, 1945, and 22
~~ American and nine French) the
~~lowing May 8.

ore French advances

~~e task of Lieutenant-General Patch
~~d the American 7th Army was to cross
~~ Rhine upstream of the 3rd Army,
~~n having gained enough ground to
~~ east, turn down towards Munich and
~~ke an assault on the "national re-
~~bt", where, according to Eisenhower's
~~elligence, Hitler would seek ultimate
~~uge. But there was no such mission in
~~re for the French 1st Army which, in
~~ initial plans, was ordered to send a
~~ps over the Rhine, following the
~~ericans, to operate in Württemberg,
~~ later a division which would start off
~~m Neuf-Brisach and occupy Baden-

Baden.

Neither General de Gaulle nor General
de Lattre accepted this view of their
intended mission. On March 4, de Gaulle
remarked to de Lattre on "reasons of
national importance that required his
army to advance beyond the Rhine";
and de Lattre expounded the plan he had
conceived to this end, which involved
moving round the Black Forest via
Stuttgart.

While de Gaulle worked on Eisenhower,
de Lattre convinced General Devers of
his point of view. The operation as conceived by de Lattre required possession
of a section of the left bank of the Rhine
below Lauterbourg; this was provided by
the dexterity with which General de
Monsabert managed to extend his II
Corps from Lauterbourg to Speyer in
the course of Operation "Undertone".

Patch moves south-east

On March 26, XV Corps of the American
7th Army managed without much trouble
to cross the Rhine at Gernsheim below
Worms. Patch exploited this success by
taking Michelstadt then, turning south,

△ *An armoured column of the
American 3rd Army pushes over
the border between Germany and
Czechoslovakia. Patton, the
army's commander, was
typically impetuous in advancing
far past his official stop line with
"deep patrols".*

he took Mannheim and Heidelberg on March 30. On April 5, having moved up the Neckar as far as Heilbronn, he captured Würzburg in the Main valley. With his left as spearhead, he hurled his forces in the direction Schweinfurt–Bamberg–Nuremberg and on April 19, after some violent fighting, ended all resistance in Munich. With its right wing in contact with the French 1st Army in the Stuttgart area, and the left in touch with the American 3rd, the 7th Army moved in a south-easterly direction. On April 25, it crossed the Danube on an 80 mile front, capturing on the way what was left of XIII Corps with its commanding officer, Lieutenant-General Count d'Oriola.

Berchtesgaden taken

From that moment German resistance in Bavaria collapsed. On May 2, the American XV Corps occupied Munich. Two days later, the French 2nd Armoured Division, once more free for assignment with the Royan pocket liquidated, scaled the slopes of the Obersalzberg and occupied the Berghof, from which *Reichsmarschall* Hermann Göring had just

fled. On the same day, the American 3[   ] Division, which had sped through Inn[   ] bruck, crossed the Brenner Pass and m[   ] up with the 88th Division of the Americ[   ] 5th Army at Vipiteno. On May 5, Gener[   ] Schulz, last commander of Army Grou[   ] "G", avoiding capture by the Frenc[   ] surrendered at General Jacob L. Devers[   ] H.Q.

On March 29, General de Gaulle te[   ] graphed de Lattre: "It is essential th[   ] you cross the Rhine even if the America[   ] are against you doing so and even if y[   ] cross in boats. It is a matter of the high[   ] national interest. Karlsruhe and Stu[   ]

In any event, the 1st Army had ceded most of its bridging equipment to the 7th Army to compensate it for similar equipment made over to the 21st Army Group; in addition, in the afternoon of March 30, the French II Corps had barely completed the relief of the American VI Corps at Germersheim and Speyer. Nevertheless, Monsabert, who was down to about 50 motorised and unmotorised boats, was ordered to take two divisions across that very night.

The venture succeeded in conditions of apparently impossible improvisation,

t are expecting you even if they don't nt you."

When he received this message, de ttre was on his way back from General vers's H.Q. with the task of sending one ps, of at least three divisions (one of m armoured), across the Rhine to e Karlsruhe, Pforzheim, and Stutt-t. De Lattre had done all in his power wring this order out of the army group mander. Pierre Lyautey remarks, on ing him in the H.Q. of the Algerian 3rd ision on March 17, that he was in the cess of conceiving "a great German mpaign", which would be "full of Napoleonic dash and fury".

△ *When the British arrived in Kiel they found the superb heavy cruiser* Admiral Hipper *there. She had spent the last months of her life supporting the army along the south coast of the Baltic Sea, but had then been heavily bombed in Kiel. She was scuttled in dock on May 3, 1945.*

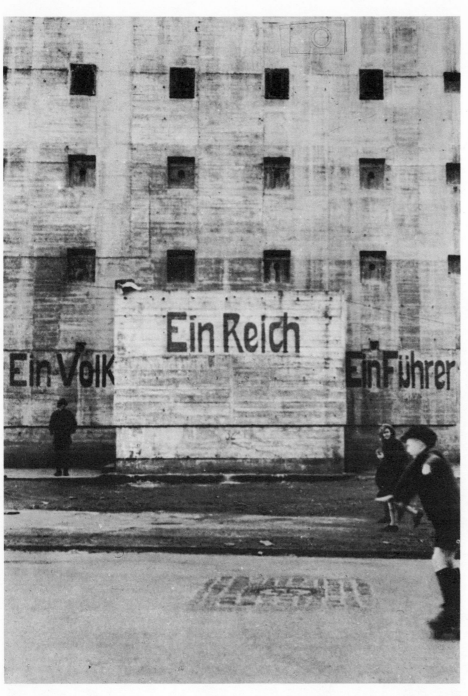

△ *An incongruous slogan in a town overrun by the Allies: "One People, one Reich, one Leader!"*

Mannheim. Finally, on April 2, the 9 Colonial Division, now under the co mand of General Valluy, crossed t river in its turn at Leimersheim (six mil south of Germersheim). Two days lat the 1st Army had taken its first objectiv Karlsruhe.

As the German 19th Army was resisti fiercely in the Neckar valley and in t hills above Rastatt, making a stand in strongly fortified position which cover the Baden-Baden plain, de Lattre shift the weight of his thrust to the centr This gave him Pforzheim on April and he then sent his 2nd Moroccan Di sion, 9th Colonial Division, and 5 Armoured Division deep into t relative wilderness of the Black Forest. (April 10, the fall of Herrenalbon and t crossing of the Murg allowed Valluy by-pass Rastatt and open the Kehl brid to General Béthouart's I Corps.

In the meantime, Monsabert had seiz Freudenstadt, the key to the Black Fore and Horb on the Neckar above Stuttga while the American VI Corps was movi up on the capital of Württemberg way of Heilbronn. On April 20, pushi on from Tübingen, the 5th Armour Division completed the encirclement the city. All resistance ceased after hours. The French took 28,000 prisone what was left of the four divisions of LX Corps (Lieutenant-General Grimeiss).

The Stuttgart manoeuvre was the thi act of this military tragedy, although April 22, the fourth act, which saw t entrance of I Corps (4th Moroccan Di sion, 9th Colonial Division, 14th Di sion, and 1st Armoured Division), w well under way. Béthouart moved Horb by way of Kehl and Oberkirc where he turned south up the Neck reaching the Swiss frontier in the vicini of Schaffhausen on the day Stuttga fell. This led to the cutting off of XV S.S. Corps (General Keppler), whi comprised four army divisions. The 40,000 Germans attempted to cut the way through the lines of the 4 Moroccan Mountain Division but th were taken in the rear by the 9th Coloni Division and on April 25 all resistan ceased.

The manoeuvre employed here by t 9th Colonial Division was the result o request made by the Swiss High Co mand – as is told in the *History of t French 1st Army* – who were understan ably not very enthusiastic about disar ing and interning thousands of alleged

and in spite of resistance from the 47th *Volksgrenadier* Division, on March 31. By nightfall, the 3rd Algerian Division (General Guillaume), opposite Speyer, and the 2nd Moroccan Division (General Carpentier), opposite Germersheim, already had five battalions in Baden-Baden. The next day, the two bridge-heads were connected and the French advanced as far as the Karlsruhe–Frankfurt *Autobahn,* over 12 miles from the right bank. As for the 5th Armoured Division (General de Vernejoul), it crossed the Rhine either by ferrying or with the co-operation of General Brooks, commanding the U.S. VI Corps, "the perfect companion in arms" in de Lattre's words, over the American bridge at

natiatical Germans. Although his plans
ere slightly put out by this development,
Lattre agreed:

"It is an obligation of another kind
give consideration to the permanent
terests of Franco-Swiss friendship,
pecially when Switzerland, while keep-
g to its age old principle of neutrality,
as always been faithful to this cause.

"The problem confronted me while
alluy was still about to attack the
aiserstuhl and Lehr's combat command
th Armoured Division) was still some
ours away from Schaffhausen. But my
esitation was only momentary. I had no
lusions as to the risks I ran but my in-
ination was on the side of Franco-Swiss
omradeship. This inspired me to issue
eneral Order No. 11 in the night April
-21, ordering I Corps to 'maintain
e drive of the right flank along the
hine towards Basle, then Waldshut,
ith simultaneous action from Schaff-
ausen towards Waldshut so as to link
p with the forces coming from Basle',
ence ensuring the complete encircle-
ent of the Black Forest and at the same

time denying the S.S. divisions any
opportunity to force the Swiss-German
frontier."

In addition, the alacrity with which
General Valluy tackled this new mission
without the slightest warning deserves
mention, Waldshut being not far short of
90 miles from the Kaiserstuhl via Lorrach.

The fifth and final act of the Rhine–
Danube campaign involved the pincer
movement carried out by Monsabert
and Béthouart on Ulm, the one with the
5th Armoured Division and 2nd Moroccan
Division (General de Linarès) to the north
of the Danube, the other thrusting his
1st Armoured Division (General Sudre)
south of the river along the line of
Donaueschingen and Biberach. On April
24 at noon, the tricolour flew above the
town which on October 21, 1805, had seen
Mack surrender his sword to Napoleon.
With the capture of Ulm a new pocket
was established, and this yielded 30,000
prisoners.

On April 29, General de Lattre
reformed I Corps, putting the 2nd Moroccan Division, the 4th Moroccan Moun-

tain Division, and the 1st and 5th Armoured Divisions under its command, and giving it the task of destroying the German 24th Army, recently formed under General Schmidt with the object of preventing the French from gaining access into the Tyrol and Vorarlberg.

On the next day the 4th Moroccan Mountain Division (General de Hesdin) and the 5th Armoured Division, of which General Schlesser had just assumed command, captured Bregenz in Austria.

Once over the frontier, the French could count on the Austrian resistance to provide guides and information, leading in numerous instances to preventing planned demolition being carried out by the Wehrmacht. At Dornbirn the tanks of the 5th Armoured Division were bombarded with bouquets of lilac; at Bludenz, which was liberated on May 4, General Schlesser was made an honorary

citizen. Meanwhile, the 2nd Morocc[an] Division and the 1st Armoured Divisi[on] were moving beyond Ulm up the vall[ey] of the Iller; from Oberstdorf General [de] Linarès's Moroccan troops scaled t[he] snow-covered slopes of the Flexenpa[ss] (5,800 feet). Nightfall on May [1] found them at Saint Anton, on the road [to] the Arlberg, having made contact wi[th] the American 44th Division on the[ir] left.

On May 7, at 1340 hours, a cease-fi[re] was declared in Austria, following Kesse[l-] ring's capitulation to General Deve[rs]. During its five weeks' campaign, t[he] French 1st Army had brought tot[al] destruction on eight German divisio[ns] and taken 180,000 prisoners. Amo[ng] these was Field-Marshal Rommel's so[n] whom de Lattre, with other consider[a-] tions than victory in mind, generous[ly] released.

▽ *Torpedoes that the Germans never had the chance to use. Although the menace of the conventional U-boat had been beaten by 1945, the Germans had high hopes of their new generation of fast Type XXI and XXIII boats. Post-war Allied evaluation of these new classes proved how dangerous such U-boats would have been.*

CHAPTER 150

The Battle of Lake Balaton

△ *The first Russian officer to enter Vienna poses in front of his Lend-Lease Sherman tank.*

In the meantime the German resistance had collapsed before the Red Army. The ring was closing round the New Chancellery in Berlin, and Vienna, the second capital of the Nazi Greater Germany, had been under Marshal Tolbukhin's control since April 13.

Between the Drava and the Carpathians, General Wöhler, commanding Army Group "South", had tried to break the Budapest blockade during the first fortnight of January. Although he had been reinforced by IV S.S. Panzer Corps, which had been withdrawn from East Prussia just before the Soviet attack on the Vistula, he failed in this attempt. The German 6th Army, which had just been transferred to General Balck's command, nevertheless managed to regain possession of the important military position of Székesfehérvár, but the effort exhausted its strength.

This setback sealed the fate of IX S.S. Mountain Corps, which, under the command of General Pfeffer-Wildenbruch, made up the Hungarian capital's garrison. On February 13, Buda castle, the defenders' last stronghold, fell to Marshal Malinovsky's troops (2nd Ukrainian Front), whilst the 3rd Ukrainian Front under Marshal Tolbukhin cleared Pest. The Russians claimed the Germans had lost 41,000 killed and 110,000 prisoners. The figures are certainly exaggerated, but nevertheless the 13th Panzer Division, the *"Feldherrnhalle"* Panzergrenadier Division, and the 33rd Hungarian S.S. Cavalry Division had been wiped out.

On March 6, the 6th *Panzerarmee*

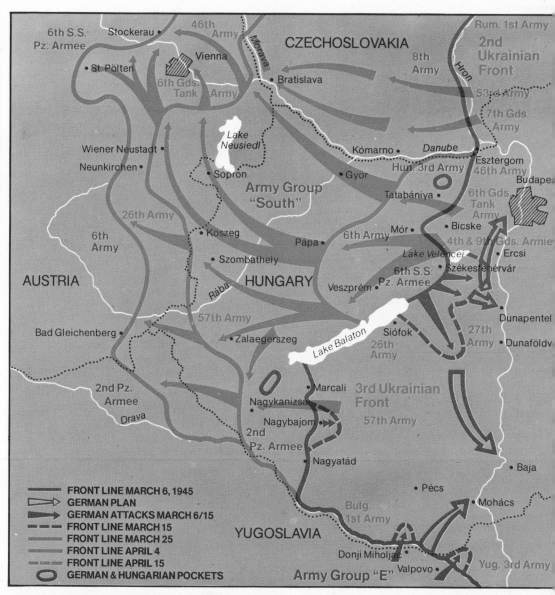

△ *Colonel-General Heinz Guderian, architect of the German* Panzerwaffe, *a very competent field commander, and lastly the O.K.H. chief-of-staff. But as chief-of-staff he had the impossible task of trying to moderate the Führer's increasingly impossible military plans, and on March 28, 1945, he was replaced by Colonel-General H. Krebs.*
▷ *Hitler's last futile offensive, the battle of Lake Balaton.*
▷▷ *The Nazi machine attacked from within: two army officers hanged for having negotiated with the Russians in Vienna.*

(Colonel-General Sepp Dietrich) went over to the offensive from the bastion of Székesfehérvár. Dietrich had left the Ardennes front on about January 25; it had taken six weeks for him to travel and take up his position. He might, on the other hand have reached the Oder front between February 5 and 10 if the plan that Guderian had vainly recommended to the Führer had been followed. The Führer in fact expected a miracle from this new offensive, indeed even the recapture of the Ploieşti oilfields.

The 3rd Ukrainian Front was to be smashed under the impact of a triple attack:

1. the left, the 6th *Panzerarmee*, consisting of eight Panzer (including the *"Leibstandarte Adolf Hitler"*, *"Das Reich"*, *"Hohenstaufen"*, and *"Hitlerjugend"*), three infantry, and two cavalry divisions, was to deliver the main blow; it was to reach the Danube at Dunaföldvar and exploit its victory

towards the south, with its left clo[se] to the Danube, its right on Lake Bal[a]ton;

2. between Lake Balaton and the Drav[a] the 2nd *Panzerarmee* (General de Ang[e]lis: six divisions) would immobili[se] Tolbukhin by attacking towar[d] Kaposzvár; and

3. on the right, Army Group "E" (Colone[l] General Löhr), in Yugoslavia, wou[ld] send a corps of three divisions acros[s] the Drava, and from Mohacs move t[o] the Danube.

The offensive of March 6 therefore co[m]mitted 22 German divisions, including [?] from Army Group "South", out of the [?] that General Wöhler had under h[is] command at the time. But this treme[n]dous effort was of no avail. On the Drav[a] and south of Lake Balaton, the Germa[n] attack collapsed after 48 hours. The ou[t]look for the 6th *Panzerarmee* seeme[d] better on the day the engagement starte[d] as the Panzers, massed on a narrow fron[t]

cceeded in breaking through, but the
orly-trained infantry proved incapable
exploiting this brief success. Tolbukhin,
the other hand, had organised his
ces in depth and countered with his
f-propelled guns. In fact, on March 12,
etrich was halted about 19 miles from
starting point, but about 16 miles from
Danube objective.

he Russian riposte

March 16, Marshals Malinovsky and
lbukhin in their turn went over to the
ack from the junction point of their two
onts. Malinovsky planned to drive the
rman 6th Army back to the Danube
ween Esztergom and Komárom,
ilst Tolbukhin, driving north-west of
kes Velencei and Balaton, intended to
it at its base the salient made in the
viet lines by the 6th *Panzerarmee*.
he 2nd Ukrainian Front's troops
l the easier task and reached their
st objective by March 21, cutting off
ir of the 6th Army's divisions.
Tolbukhin, on the other hand, met such
n resistance on March 16 and 17 from
S.S. Panzer Corps, forming Balck's
ht, that the *Stavka* put the 6th Guards
nk Army at his disposal. However,
ause of Malinovsky's success, Wöhler
ok two Panzer divisions from the 6th
nzerarmee and set them against Mali-
vsky's forces. As the inequality between
ack and defence became increasingly
rked, Dietrich managed to evacuate
salient he had captured between
rch 6 and 12, and then on March 24
brought his troops back through the
tleneck at Székesfehérvár. But what
saved from the trap was merely a
chpotch of worn-out men with neither
pplies nor equipment.
On March 27, the 6th Guards Tank
my was at Veszprém and Devecser,
and 48 miles from its starting point.
March 29, Tolbukhin crossed the
ba at Sárvár, and Malinovsky crossed
at Györ, where it meets the Danube.
e Hungarian front had therefore
lapsed; this was not surprising as
hler, who had no reserves, had had 11
nzer divisions more or less destroyed
ween March 16 and 27.
On April 6 Hitler, consistent in his
sjudgement, stripped Wöhler of com-
nd of Army Group "South" and gave
o Colonel-General Rendulic, whom he

The British Supermarine Spitfire XIVE fighter and fighter-bomber

Engine: one Rolls-Royce Griffon 65 inline, 2,050-hp.
Armament: two 20-mm Hispano cannon with 120 rounds per gun and two .5-inch Browning machine guns with 250 rounds per gun, plus one 500-lb and two 250-lb bombs.
Speed: 448 mph at 26,000 feet.
Climb: 7 minutes to 20,000 feet.
Ceiling: 44,500 feet.
Range: 850 miles with drop tanks.
Weight empty/loaded: 6,600/ 8,500 lbs.
Span: 36 feet 10 inches.
Length: 32 feet 8 inches.
Height: 12 feet 8½ inches.

ecalled from the Kurland pocket for the ask.

Vienna falls

ut Malinovsky had already driven etween Lake Neusiedl and the Danube n April 2, and had forced the Leitha at ruck, whilst Tolbukhin, who had cap- ured the large industrial centre of Wiener eustadt, launched one column along he Semmering road towards Graz and nother towards Mödling and Vienna. he day he took over his command, endulic was informed that the advance uard of the 3rd Ukrainian Front was ready in Klosterneuburg north of ienna, and that the 2nd Ukrainian Front as already approaching it from the outh. A week later, a cease-fire was gned in the famous Prater Park, but addition to the ordeal of a week's street ghting, the wretched Viennese still had suffer much brutality and shameless oting from their "liberators".

Tolbukhin, who boasted of the capture of 130,000 prisoners, 1,350 tanks, and 2,250 guns, went up the right bank of the Danube, but his main forces did not go further than Amstetten, a small town 75 miles west of Vienna. On May 4, his patrols in the outskirts of Linz met a reconnaissance unit of the U.S. 3rd Army, and on the same day made contact with the advance guard of the British 8th Army on the Graz road. After helping to clear Vienna, Malinovsky sent his armies on the left across the Danube in the direction of Moravia. At Mikulov they crossed the pre-Munich (1938) Austro- Czechoslovak frontier. On the left bank of the Danube, the right wing of the 2nd Ukrainian Front, including the Rumanian 1st and 4th Armies (Generals Atanasiu and Dascalesco), liberated Slovakia and then, converging towards the north-west, occupied Brno on April 24 and were close to Olomouc when hostilities ceased. Slovakia's administration was handed over to the representatives of the Czecho- slovak government-in-exile under Eduard Beneš as the occupation proceeded. On

▽ *Russian T-34/85 medium tanks move through an Austrian village in the closing days of the war.*

△ The Allies meet in Austria: Marshal of the Soviet Union F. I. Tolbukhin salutes General George S. Patton Jr.

General Guderian viewed the matte differently; urging Himmler to tak soundings in Stockholm for surrende he repeated several times: "It's no 11.55 now – it's 12.05!" In view of the ope pessimism of his O.K.H. Chief-of-Staf Hitler dismissed him on March 28 o grounds of ill health and appointe Colonel-General H. Krebs, who had bee the German military attaché in Mosco on June 22, 1941, as his successor.

Army Group "Vistula" was charge with the defence of Berlin; Heinric Himmler had just been replaced b Colonel-General Gotthard Heinrici, wh rightly enjoyed the complete confidenc of his staff and his troops. Corneliu Ryan's judgement seems quite correc "A thoughtful, precise strategist, deceptively mild-mannered commande Heinrici was nevertheless a tough gener: of the old aristocratic school who ha long ago learned to hold the line with th minimum of men and at the lowest possib cost."

Heinrici was in contact with Arm Group "Centre" a little below Gube on the Neisse, and was in control of th Oder front between Fürstenberg ar Stettin, but the 1st Belorussian Front o both sides of Küstrin already had a wic bridgehead on the left bank of the rive

The German 9th Army, under Gener Busse, had the special mission of barrir the invader's path to Berlin. It was acco dingly deployed between Guben and th Hohenzollern Canal connecting th Oder and the Havel:

1. V S.S. Mountain Corps (337th, 32r "*Freiwilligen*" S.S. Grenadier, ar 236th Divisions) under Gener Jeckeln;
2. Frankfurt garrison of one divisio
3. XI S.S. Panzer Corps ("*Müncheber*, Panzer, 712nd, 169th, and 9th Parachu Divisions) under General M. Klei heisterkamp;
4. XCI Corps (309th "Berlin", 303 "*Döberitz*", 606th, and 5th *Jäger* Di sion) under General Berlin.

This gave a total of 12 divisions on ε 80 mile front. Busse, on the other han had kept the "*Kurmark*" Panzer Divisic in reserve on the Frankfurt axis and th 25th Panzer Division on the Küstrin ax

The 3rd *Panzerarmee* was deploy between the Hohenzollern and Stett canal; on a 95-mile front it had about t divisions incorporated in XLVI Panz Corps, XXXII Corps, and the 3rd Mari Division.

the other hand, Stalin seized Ruthenia in the lower Carpathian mountains; it had never even been a part of the Tsarist empire.

The defence of Berlin

On March 10, 1945, Hitler told Kessel-ring that he viewed the offensive Stalin was preparing to launch against Berlin with complete confidence. Colonel-

The British Cruiser Tank Mark VIII Cromwell VI

Weight: 27.5 tons.
Armament: one 95-mm Tank Howitzer
Mark I and two 7.92-mm Besa machine guns.
Armour: hull front 63-mm, glacis 30-mm,
nose 57-mm, sides 32-mm, decking 20-mm,
belly 8-mm, and rear 32-mm; turret front
76-mm, sides 63-mm, rear 57-mm, and
roof 20-mm.
Engine: one Rolls-Royce Meteor inline,
600-hp.
Speed: 38 mph.
Range: 173 miles on roads, 81 miles
cross-country.
Length: 20 feet 10 inches (hull).
Width: 10 feet.
Height: 8 feet 3 inches.

Heinrici kept his 18th *Panzergrenadier*, 11th *"Nordland"* S.S. *Freiwilligen Panzergrenadier*, and 23rd *"Nederland"* S.S. *Freiwilligen Panzergrenadier* Divisions, composed of Norwegian, Danish, Dutch, and Belgian volunteers.

Finally, O.K.H. kept control of XXXIX Panzer Corps, but as Hitler's intuition told him that the Russians' main attack would be directed not against Berlin, but along the Görlitz–Dresden–Prague axis, he handed over this corps to Field-Marshal Schörner and put LVI Panzer Corps, which was considerably weaker, in the rear of Army Group "Vistula".

Roosevelt dies

On April 12, Franklin Roosevelt's sudden death seemed to Hitler like a long awaited and providential miracle, comparable in every respect to the divine intervention which had eliminated the Tsarina Elizbeth and saved Frederick II, who had beeon the point of taking poison at the wormoment of the Seven Years' War. Hitlthought he would not only defeat tRussians at the gates of Berlin, but ththe English, American, and Soviet forcwould become inextricably confusedMecklenburg and Saxony, German guwould fire themselves, and he wouremain master of the situation.

The Russians, according to the messasent to Eisenhower by Stalin, were usionly "secondary forces" against Berin this last battle of the war on the EasteFront. These "secondary forces" totalat least three army groups or fronconsisting of 20 armies, 41,000 mortaand guns, 6,300 tanks, and 8,400 planin the attack, which started at 0400 houon April 16. On the 1st Belorussian Fronwhich broadly speaking was facing tGerman 9th Army, Marshal Zhukov haten armies: 3rd and 5th Shock Armie8th Guards Army (General V. I. Chuikov1st and 2nd Guards Tank Armi(Generals M. E. Katukov and S. I. Bodanov), the 1st Polish Army (GenerS. G. Poplavsky), and the 61st, 47th, 8tand 33rd Armies. He also had eig

▽ *Russian armour/infantry attack. Note the man at the left, carrying a mortar base plate.*

tillery divisions and General S. I. denko's 16th Air Army. His task was encircle and take Berlin.

On Zhukov's right, Marshal I. S. nev's 1st Ukrainian Front contained ven armies: 3rd and 5th Guards Armies enerals V. N. Gordov and A. S. Zhadov), and 4th Guards Tank Armies (Colonel-neral P. S. Rybalko and General D. Lelyushenko) 2nd Polish Army eneral K. Swierczewski), and 13th and nd Armies. He also had seven artillery visions and Colonel-General K. A. ershinin's 4th Air Army. After forcing e Neisse, Konev was to exploit his ctory along the Bautzen–Dresden axis, t in case Zhukov's thrust slowed down, was to be prepared to converge his bile troops on Berlin and take part in e encirclement and assault on the city.

To the right of Zhukov, the 2nd Belo-ssian Front (Marshal K. K. Rokossov-y) had five armies (2nd Shock, and 19th, th, 70th, and 49th) with four tank or chanised corps, and Colonel-General A. Krasovsky's 2nd Air Army. On ril 20, Rokossovsky was to attack on e Schwedt–Neustrelitz axis, drive the

3rd *Panzerarmee* to the Baltic, and link up with Field-Marshal Montgomery's forces. Although Telpukhovsky as usual does not state the number of Soviet divisions taking part in this campaign, they may be assessed at 140 divisions or their equivalent. The Germans had 37 weakened divisions to take the first blow, including the 4th *Panzerarmee*, which faced the 1st Ukrainian Front on the Neisse. Another difficulty was caused by the fact that the defence was extremely short of fuel and munitions, and the German troops were seriously undertrained. Moreover, as Telpukhovsky points out, Soviet planes had complete air supremacy. Busse, for instance, only had 300 fighters, all desperately short of fuel, to oppose Zhukov's 16th Air Army.

The final appeal

As Zhukov and Konev started the attack, the German troops were handed out Adolf Hitler's last order of the day, which included the following passages:

The End in Germany

Rügen
Stralsund
Peenemünde
Rostock • Greifswald • Usedom • Treptow
Wismar • Güstrow • X S.S. Corps
21st Army • Demmin • Swinemünde
Schwerin • Anklam • Wollin • 19th Army • 2nd
Br. 2nd GERMANY 3rd Pz. Armee Belorussian
Army Neubrandenburg XXXII Front
Ludwigslust • Neustrelitz Szczecin 2nd Shock Army
Army Group "Vistula" Prenzlau
• Pritzwalk XLVI Pz. 65th Army
Elbe • Wittenberge Havel Templin Corps 70th Army
Neuruppin Schwedt 49th Army
U.S. 9th Hohenzollern Canal LI Corps 61st Army POLAND
Army Oranienburg Eberswalde Pol. 1st Army 1st
Stendal • Rathenow • Prötzel 47th Army Belorussian
Berlin 3rd Shock Army Front
Brandenburg • Potsdam Manenfelde 5th Shock Army 2nd Gds.
Magdeburg Zossen 9th Army Furstenwalde 8th Gds. Army Tank
12th Army XI S.S. Corps 69th Army Army
Lückenwalde V S.S. Corps Frankfurt 3rd Army
Baruth 33rd Army 1st Gds.
Lübben V Corps Eisenhüttenstadt Tank Army
Luckau Guben Oder
Spree 4th Pz. Armee
U.S. 1st Cottbus 1st Ukrainian Front
Army Saale Mulde 4th Pz. Finsterwalde 3rd Gds. Army
Leipzig Armee Spremberg 3rd & 4th Gds. Tank
Meissen 13th Army Armies
Bautzen 5th Gds. Army
Görlitz Pol. 2nd Army
7th Army • Dresden 52nd Army
Army Group LVII Pz. Corps
"Centre" 17th
CZECHOSLOVAKIA Army

FRONT LINE ON APRIL 16
FRONT LINE ON APRIL 18
U.S. 3rd Army
FRONT LINE ON APRIL 25
FRONT LINE ON MAY 8
GERMAN POCKETS
GERMAN COUNTER-ATTACKS
GERMAN DEFENCE LINES

△ *The Allies crush Germany.*
▷ *Russian armour on the move.*

"For the last time, the deadly Jewish Bolshevik enemy has started a mass attack. He is trying to reduce Germany to rubble and to exterminate our people. Soldiers of the East! You are already fully aware now of the fate that threatens German women and children. Whilst men, children, and old people will be murdered, women and girls will be reduced to the rôle of barrack-room whores. The rest will be marched off to Siberia.

But the Führer had provided the means to put a stop to this terrible assault; everything was ready for meeting it, and the outcome now depended on the tenacity of the German soldiers. He therefore wrote: "If every soldier does his duty on the Eastern Front in the days and weeks to come, Asia's last attack will be broken as surely as the Western enemy's invasion will in spite of everything finally fail.

"Berlin will remain German. Vienna will become German again and Europe will never be Russian!"

At the same time the Soviet soldiers in the line were told: "The time has come to free our fathers, mothers, brothers, sisters, wives, and children still languishing under the Fascist yoke in Germany. The time has come to draw up the balance sheet of the abominable crimes perpetrated on our soil by the Hitlerite cannibals and to punish those responsible for these atrocities. The time has come to inflict the final defeat on the enemy and to draw this war to a victorious conclusion."